# STORIES *That* TRANSFORM

A fresh look at the parables of Jesus

Published by the Review and Herald® Publishing Association, Silver Spring, MD 20904

The Review and Herald® Publishing Association publishes biblically based materials for spiritual, physical, and mental growth and Christian discipleship.

Bible texts are from the New King James Version®. Copyright © 1982 by Thomas Nelson. Used by permission. All rights reserved.

This book was

Edited and copyedited by James Cavil
Cover illustration by © rudall30/Adobe Stock
Cover design by Stein Vegard Halvorsen
Back cover image by Per Arild Struksnes
Interior design by Melinda Worden
Typeset: 12/14 Bembo

Stories That Transform

PRINTED IN THE U.S.A.

ISBN   978-0-8280-2944-5 (print)
        978-0-8127-0575-1 (ebook)
        978-0-8127-0576-8 (audio)

# STORIES *That* TRANSFORM

A fresh look at the parables of Jesus

Daniel Pel

**Review&Herald®**
PUBLISHING ASSOCIATION

SINCE 1861 | **REVIEWANDHERALD.COM**
SILVER SPRING, MARYLAND

# ENDORSEMENTS

Daniel Pel allows the parables of Jesus to speak to life's toughest questions about human suffering, the meaning of life, the character of God, and how a person can receive eternal life. Though the message of the parables is hidden behind metaphorical language, Stories That Transform uses the Bible to make the meaning unmistakably clear. Young and old will feel convicted, challenged, and encouraged by the surprising insights gained from these symbolic teachings of Jesus.

—Joe Reeves, editor, *in Verse*

This is a lovely book. It explains the stories of Jesus in simple easy-to-read language and applies the principles of Jesus' teaching to the everyday life of the reader. In explaining the parables, Daniel Pel uses stories from his own life and the lives of others, making this book accessible and relatable. Take time to read this book, and you will gain new insights into the parables and their importance to the lives of all who seek to know God.

—Victor Marley, president, Norwegian Union, Seventh-day Adventist Church

I have known Daniel Pel for almost 20 years. This book is the result of his close encounter with Jesus, studying the Word, and many blessed experiences ministering to people around the globe. You will find the 12 chapters easy to read and helpful in your walk with God. I highly recommend this book and pray it will draw you nearer to Him!

—Jan Harry Cabungcal, neuroscientist/assistant to AWR president for global evangelism

Using engaging narratives and parables, Daniel has brilliantly weaved in doctrinal truths applicable to our present time. He has taken well-known parables and made them highly applicable to the Christian journey.

—Johnny Wong, church planter, author of *Business Unusual*, Melbourne, Australia

In Stories That Transform, Daniel Pel has made Jesus' parables extremely practical and compelling, yet deeply thought-provoking. Daniel urges us to "find ourselves" in each parable and allow the words of Christ to transform us. Not only does he present fresh insights in each individual parable, but the developments and connections between the parables paint a fascinating story we are invited to be part of. If you want to explore Jesus' parables for the first time or anew, this book is for you!

—Cody Francis, Ministerial director, Michigan Conference

# DEDICATION

"To my wife, Silvia, who has walked every step of this journey with me"

"To my young sons, Elias and Enoch, who faithfully prayed for Daddy's book"

And…

"For every reader who finds their story within these pages"

# PREFACE

Jesus Christ was no doubt the greatest teacher this world has ever known. When He spoke, people were amazed and astonished at His teaching. His words reached men and women of all ages. People flocked to hear Him speak. Both the rich and the poor, the educated and the uneducated, found something in His instructions that touched the deepest chords of their hearts. Ever since Jesus left this world, His words have continued to impact generation after generation. Throughout the past 2,000 years of human history, the Gospel accounts, containing the teachings of Jesus, have inspired and shaped the lives of millions of people. This is really no surprise, as the words of Jesus were carefully crafted and designed in the very heart of a God of love. A God who spoke and it came to be. A God who created human beings and placed within them a longing for words of truth.

In a world that had fallen into sin and been separated from its maker, Jesus came to reveal the loving character of God to humanity. To reach the sinful heart, which was barricaded by pride and selfishness, Jesus sought to call people's attention to the principles that govern true happiness. Through practical illustrations and stories Jesus drew people into a new world in which healing and restoration could take place. Jesus called this new reality His kingdom. It is a kingdom in which love for God and love for others is central. Everyone is invited, but Jesus made it plain that not everyone would want to be a citizen of this new kingdom.

The parables of Jesus are not cute little stories with gentle suggestions for improving our lives. Jesus was launching a radical new way of living that operates by principles and relational dynamics that confront the ways of this world. His teachings challenge us to take a deeper look at our priorities and what matters most in life.

Stories have a way of conveying difficult things in a relatable way. It was through parables that Jesus explained what His kingdom was like. Jesus used illustrations from everyday life, to paint a graphic picture of what it meant to follow Him and live in harmony with God. Parable teaching was popular and commanded the respect and attention of both Jews and people of other nations. The word "parable" means to "cast alongside." It's a story alongside a spiritual truth. The story provides an avenue to explore the spiritual reality more deeply. The core truths of His kingdom were packaged in such a way that people from a wide variety of backgrounds could find purpose and meaning in His words. And so it is today! The parables of Jesus continue to shape the lives of people around the world.

As you read and study these transformative stories, you will be both inspired and challenged. Inspired by the mind-blowing beauty of the gospel story and challenged by the need to let Jesus change you from within. The parables of Jesus cover a wide range of topics, though they all center in the overarching theme of revealing what the kingdom of God is really like. In contrast to the way of life, there is a way that leads to death. The parables of Jesus warn us about this destructive road and remind us of the great controversy between good and evil that is raging in this universe. When all is said and done, there are only two sides in this cosmic conflict.

The parables engage both our mind and heart, uncovering what really matters in this life and in eternity. Jesus reveals what will last when the great storm, predicted in prophecy, sweeps across this world before Jesus comes back the second time to establish His final kingdom of glory. The transformational teachings of Jesus, revealed in the parables, prepare us for His coming. Scripture culminates in a wedding, as Jesus, portrayed as our bridegroom, comes to take us, His bride, to a place He has prepared for us. It's a love story you don't want to miss!

So before we dive into this love story, I should probably let you know how this book came to be. I am not a seasoned writer by any definition. Though I enjoy writing, this is my first published book. My primary method of communication has been preaching and teaching. For the past 20 years my passion for the gospel has led me to share with audiences around the world. On one of these trips I visited the campus of Bogenhofen, a Christian academy and seminary, in the beautiful country of Austria. For a week I preached and taught on the parables of Jesus. Toward the end of the week I was contacted by the editor of In-Verse, a young adult study guide used by the Adventist Church worldwide. I was asked if I could write a study guide quarterly on the parables. Putting my sermon concepts into writing was a rewarding process that I enjoyed. The natural next step was putting this material into a book. Though writing a book is a daunting task, it is also fulfilling. I can´t think of a greater joy than sharing with others what has meant most to me.

Let's prayerfully embark on this journey together. It's going to be both exhilarating and challenging. May the stories that have literally changed the lives of millions make a difference in your existence today. You are no accident—you were made for a purpose. Let Jesus, the greatest teacher, reveal to you what this purpose is.

Daniel Pel

# CONTENTS

# Chapter 1

# THE SECRET TO SPIRITUAL GROWTH

The Parable of the Sower | Based on Mark 4:1-9

*e have been robbed*! The words still echo through my mind. It was dark and we had no electricity, so I felt my way through the room. We were far from home, on our first mission trip, in East Africa. Others in our team had also woken up, and together we assessed what had just happened. A few men had broken into the house we were staying in and robbed us of our equipment and belongings. Luckily, we were unharmed. We had just concluded several weeks of gospel preaching, and this was our last night at this location. The plan was to travel to a new place for several more weeks of ministry. Now everything was in disarray, and we had no idea what to do.

I don´t want to pretend I am some spiritual superhero. My first thought was that it was time to go home. We had tried the missionary life, and it wasn't exactly what we had anticipated. It didn´t match with the glorified stories we had heard. What we see in mission reports is only one side of the story. Masses of people receiving Jesus into their lives, baptisms, glowing testimonies, and perfect smiles with the backdrop of a magnificent African sunset is an alluring incentive to join. But getting robbed was not what we had signed up for. Questions filled my mind as I tried to make sense of it all. Why us? Why now?

At moments like this, close friends are priceless. One of our team members started sharing about the apostle Paul, whose life we can follow in the New Testament. We are told that he suffered shipwreck, was beaten on multiple occasions, and would have likely been robbed at some point on all his journeys in the first-century Mediterranean world. However, nothing seemed to stop him from moving forward as he continued to raise up churches throughout the Roman Empire. At one point he was thrown into prison for preaching the gospel, but even this dark dungeon couldn't quell his passion to share Jesus. Together with his friend and colaborer Silas, he started singing songs in the middle of the night. This, combined with a miraculous intervention, led to the conversion of the jailer.

As these stories swirled through my mind, I realized that we couldn't just leave once trials hit us. So we decided to press on and complete our intended trip, which meant a few more weeks of preaching in a new location. There was just one big problem. Everything I needed to preach a series of meetings was gone. I had been using PowerPoint slides, but my laptop and projector had been stolen. The thieves had even taken all my sermon notes and my precious Bible! I did hope they would read them. But how could I preach without all this? I wrestled with God and told Him that He would need to do something supernatural if this was going to work. Sometimes we simply need to come to the end of ourselves to recognize that our strength does not come from within us but from above.

I am often reminded of the words of Jesus to the apostle Paul when He said: *"My grace is sufficient for you, for My strength is made perfect in weakness"* (2 Corinthians 12:9).

In our world our strength is revealed in our money, our possessions, and our careers. It is seen in our knowledge and is displayed in the people we associate with and those we don't want to be seen around. But God's kingdom is an upside-down kingdom. It is one that is accessed only when we become dependent on a source of power that is outside of us.

I will never forget that day, after the robbery, when a faithful friend put a pocket Bible in my hand and reassured me that David slew Goliath with a little stone! Equipped with nothing more than a borrowed Bible, but filled with God's Spirit, I got up night after night to proclaim the gospel. By God's grace we saw many precious people turn to Jesus and get baptized. Something supernatural was truly taking place, and I know till this day that it was not because of anything I had produced, since all of that had been stripped away. This experience showed me that when we simply trust and depend on God's Word, it will do what it has promised.

Through Isaiah God assures us: *"So shall My word be that goes forth from My mouth; It shall not return to Me void, but it shall accomplish what I please, and it shall prosper in the thing for which I sent it"* (Isaiah 55:11).

There is not a single verse in the Bible that I have prayed more often than this one. Each time before I get up to preach, I claim this promise. God's Word has the power to transform lives.

## THE KEY TO UNDERSTANDING THE PARABLES

In this first chapter we are going to look at a parable that reveals the power of the Word and how it can have the greatest effect in our lives. Jesus told a parable about a sower who went out to sow seed. The seed in the parable is a picture of God's Word. Some of the seed falls on good soil, sprouts up, and eventually produces fruit. This is exactly what Jesus wants His words, His teaching, to accomplish in our lives. The fruit of God's Word provides us with a purpose, true happiness, and a hope that this world cannot offer. In many ways this story is the parable that unlocks all other parables. It is the key to understanding the mysteries of God's kingdom. But, as we will discover, there are things that can hinder the entrance of these words of life.

Imagine the scene as Jesus looked at the vast crowd of people that had gathered to hear Him teach. All kinds of people had come to listen to this popular young Rabbi, and as the people pressed in on Jesus, He decided to get into a boat. He asked His disciples to push off a little from the land, so He could address the multitude.

As He began speaking about a sower who went forth to sow, the people would have been able to see this scene played out on the hills and in the surrounding plains. Everyone knew how important it was for the seed to land in fertile ground for it to sprout and bear fruit. But not everyone present was aware of how the very words of Jesus were a type of seed that was right now landing in the soil of their lives. The parable reveals how the words and teachings of Jesus would be received. Just as the sower spreads the seed, so Jesus was spreading and sharing words of life.

In the parable Jesus described how the seed of the sower fell in different places.

*"Listen! Behold, a sower went out to sow. And it happened, as he sowed, that some seed fell by the wayside; and the birds of the air came and devoured it. Some fell on stony ground, where it did not have much earth; and immediately it sprang up because it had no depth of earth. But when the sun was up it was scorched, and because it had no root it withered away. And some seed fell among thorns; and the thorns grew up and choked it, and it yielded no crop. But other seed fell on good ground and yielded a crop that sprang up, increased and produced: some thirtyfold, some sixty, and some a hundred"* (Mark 4:3-8).

Later that day Jesus' closest disciples probed Him, seeking for an understanding of the story they had heard. As Jesus explained the parable to them, He identified three places the seed was not able to grow and bear fruit. He was pointing to things that hinder God's Word from having the effect it is designed to have in us.

*"The sower sows the word. And these are the ones by the wayside where the word is sown. When they hear, Satan comes immediately and takes away the word that was sown in their hearts. These likewise are the ones sown on stony ground who, when they hear the word, immediately receive it with gladness; and they have no root in themselves, and so endure only for a time. Afterward, when tribulation or persecution arises for the word's sake, immediately they stumble. Now these are the ones sown among thorns; they are the ones who hear the word, and the cares of this world, the deceitfulness of riches, and the desires for other things entering in choke the word, and it becomes unfruitful"* (verses 14-19).

There is something that these three scenarios have in common. The seed does not have the time to develop into a plant that bears fruit. On the wayside it is immediately removed. On the stony ground it endures for a short time, and among the thorns it endures longer, but is eventually choked.

## DIFFERENT SOIL

The wayside response occurs when the teaching goes into one ear and out the other. Perhaps you can relate to this. Have you ever read a chapter in a book, only to realize that your thoughts were in a completely different place, and now you hardly have a clue about what you just read? Or perhaps you are attending a class or lecture, but suddenly you are aware that although your body was present, your mind wasn´t. Most married couples will be able to relate to the fact that sometimes your spouse is hearing you but not actually hearing you. We pick up sound, but we are not registering and seeking to understand what our spouse is communicating. It is said that one of the most difficult things in life is to actively listen and comprehend what someone is saying to us. It appears that we are living in a day and age in which our attention span is as short as it ever has been. And yet Jesus knew something that communication experts have discovered again and again. Whatever has our attention has us!

The Scriptures disclose a real battle between good and evil. Jesus, in the parable, reveals who removes the seed from the wayside. He is called Satan, and no – he is not the little red dragon with the pitchfork. This caricature, passed down from medieval art, makes the whole idea of a tempter ludicrous. But when we allow the biblical narrative itself to unmask this figure, we gain an insight into who he really is. He is displayed as a glorious angel who rebelled against his maker, God (Isaiah 14:12-14). He is described as stunningly beautiful, and yet deceptive at heart (Ezekiel 28:13-15). His goal is to make war on God as he seeks to misrepresent Him before angels and humans. No wonder he is trying desperately to snatch away the seed of God's Word. How does he do this? He seeks to catch our attention and move it to anything else possible. It does not really matter what it is, as long as it is not the words of Jesus.

While the wayside response depicts the shortest attention span, the seed on the stony ground survives a little bit longer. However, it has no place to develop roots, and endures only until there is opposition. In the famous classic *Pilgrim's Progress*, an allegory on our journey to heaven, there is a character named Pliable. He is enticed by Christian's description of the glories of the celestial city, but as soon as the first obstacle occurs at the Slough of Despond, Pliable leaves Christian. He has this memorable line: "I have no problem changing my mind." Resistance to God's Word often comes when obeying and following His Word becomes challenging.

The thorny ground is the saddest of all. Just as the thorns and thistles slowly enwrap the precious plant, so the cares of this world slowly choke out the Word. It does not happen overnight. It happens gradually, when we lose our first love for God and our love is channeled to the things of this world. Something else has our main attention. Eventually there is no more interest left for that which was once most important. The fact that you are reading this book reveals that you are seeking after a greater understanding of the teachings of Jesus. However, we all feel the pull of the world around us. We are continually bombarded with worldviews and ideologies that seek to contradict the words of Jesus in so many areas. We were all made to worship, and when we don't worship God, we will eventually worship something else. If Jesus is not our treasure, something else will be.

We will come back to this idea in a future chapter.

## GROWTH POTENTIAL

To avoid these pitfalls, we need to let Jesus cultivate our hearts, making sure we are good ground. To have good soil, you need a good composition of nutrients. Many factors are involved in making a type of soil that is either receiving the seed or rejecting it. The same is true in our spiritual lives. The make-up of our "soil" results in how effective the seed of the Word is—*"some thirtyfold, some sixty, and some a hundred"* (verse 20).

There are certain things about our environment that we have no control over, such as the place and circumstances of our up-bringing. However, later in life we can to a degree choose and create the environment we consider best. We choose our friends, interests, and values. We decide what principles we believe are best to follow. As an adult, you have more control over "your soil" than you had as a child. When you place yourself in a good environment and make choices that prioritize a wholistic spiri-tual development, the seed of God's Word has a lot more poten-tial to bear fruit.

I have seen people in a short time make huge life-altering choices that have propelled them in a certain direction. As a pas-tor I have had the privilege of having a front seat when it comes to the effect of God's Word on a person. I have seen marriag-es restored and relationships healed. I have witnessed people move from a life of depression and despair to one of purpose and meaning. Suddenly a light is switched on, and a process of restoration begins. These precious moments never fail to im-press me with the power of the Word. But I know that there is more than the Word at play here. There is the soil. The heart of every man and woman. The Word always has power wherever it lands, but it will make a difference only when the soil is good. I have preached the same sermons in different places and yet seen remarkable differences in how they were received and applied. This parable is not just an interesting story; it is a reality that repeats itself every time God's Word is proclaimed.

It's interesting that even on the good soil there is a different outcome, as some produces *"thirtyfold, some sixty, and some a hun-dred."* Again, the diverse outcome is not based on the seed, as it is the same wherever it falls. It's the soil that makes the difference!

There is good soil, better soil, and the best soil. I don't want to settle for anything less than the best. If you agree, stay tuned as each parable of Jesus reveals how we can be the best soil possible.

The journey has begun, and we have set our course. We have discovered the secret for all spiritual development. It's a simple equation: the power of the Word + the best soil = spiritual growth and fruit. Don´t underestimate this powerful truth. It´s available to all who are willing to hear.

Jesus ends this foundational parable with the words:

*"He who has ears to hear, let him hear!"* (Mark 4:9).

I am confident that this is describing you. See you in the next chapter!

# Chapter 2

# LOST BUT FOUND

The Parables of the Lost Sheep, Coin, and Son

Based on Luke 15:1-32

Have you ever lost something of great emotional value? A lot of things in this world can be replaced, but there are certain items that simply can't. Such as a wedding ring, reminding you of the most important day in your life. Or an old photograph of your childhood, bringing back sweet memories. Or perhaps a special souvenir, connecting you to distant places. Once such an item is lost, it is almost as if part of our lives are missing. But more important than any item or object are people. When people go missing, enormous efforts are made to find them. There seems to be no limit for what we are willing to spend in time, money, and effort to find our loved one. Many parents have felt the panic of losing sight of their young child. Fortunately, it usually does not take long before the child is found again, after wandering down the street or through the mall.

My wife and I had such an experience at a conference we organized. Both of us were busy talking to people, and suddenly our 2-year-old was gone. We quickly ran to the nearby lake to make sure he hadn't fallen into the water. After a few minutes we had many of the campers join the search. It took only a few more minutes before we found our boy peacefully strolling through one of the rooms after he had climbed some stairs. We had a huge sense of relief and joy the moment we saw him.

## PURSUED BY GOD'S GOODNESS

Jesus held His audience spellbound as He told them a story

about a lost son, or, more precisely, two lost sons, as we will discover. These sons were lost by their own choices. In this parable the heart of the gospel is on full display as we encounter a God in pursuit of humanity. Jesus came to seek and save the lost, and this includes each of us.

But before we get to the famous parable of the prodigal son, Jesus tells two other stories about something that got lost but was found. The parables that Jesus told are not just interesting stories. As the title of this book suggests, they are "*stories that transform.*" For these stories to change us, we need to be able to find ourselves in them. The three stories we find in the gospel of Luke 15 are really tapping into the fate of all humanity. We are all lost in sin and need to be found by God. These fascinating stories picture the different ways we can be lost.

In the first story Jesus talks about a sheep that got lost and needed to be found.

*"What man of you, having a hundred sheep, if he loses one of them, does not leave the ninety-nine in the wilderness, and go after the one which is lost until he finds it? And when he has found it, he lays it on his shoulders, rejoicing. And when he comes home, he calls together his friends and neighbors, saying to them, 'Rejoice with me, for I have found my sheep which was lost!' I say to you that likewise there will be more joy in heaven over one sinner who repents than over ninety-nine just persons who need no repentance"* (Luke 15:4-7).

The sheep realized it was lost, but could not find its way back. Many people can find themselves in this story. They know there is something lacking in their lives and are full of unanswered questions. They feel "lost" in life and are looking around, hoping to find some way out of this conundrum. However, they don't know where to find their purpose and identity. They are waiting to be found. This sense of perceiving that there is something more is there only because God put it there in the first place.

*"He has made everything beautiful in its time. Also He has put eternity in their hearts"* (Ecclesiastes 3:11).

God put a longing for eternity inside each person born into

this world. This is why we intuitively know that there must be something more than the life we see and experience on the surface. This longing is often pushed away or replaced, but for many life remains an unsolved mystery. The idea that we are here merely because of cosmology and biology is not satisfying. There must be something more.

According to the Scriptures, God not only put a longing for something more in our hearts but also actively revealed Himself to us. The apostle Paul alluded to this when he addressed a crowd of Athenians in Greece. They were stooped in idol worship, but somehow no idol, god, or goddess could satisfy their search for truth. Paul, with a clever twist, pointed this out.

*"Then Paul stood in the midst of the Areopagus and said, 'Men of Athens, I perceive that in all things you are very religious; for as I was passing through and considering the objects of your worship, I even found an altar with this inscription: TO THE UNKNOWN GOD. Therefore, the One whom you worship without knowing, Him I proclaim to you"* (Acts 17:22, 23).

The very fact that the Athenians had raised this altar with this very inscription indicates that they believed there was something, or rather someone, they were still not familiar with. Paul seeks to bridge this gap. He wants them to be found by the one and only true God. This is possible because God has revealed Himself. Paul reminds them that *"He is not far from each one of us"* (verse 27).

Throughout Scripture we encounter an active God who is pursuing people, revealing Himself to them. From the very beginning, when sin entered the world, we see the first human beings hide from God, but He seeks them and finds them. He restores them with promises of a coming Messiah who will make all things right.

No doubt the shepherd who finds the sheep in our story is none other than Jesus Himself. So if Jesus is our shepherd and we are the lost sheep, what do we do? We simply allow ourselves to be found. When He reveals Himself to us, we rejoice in the fact that in Him all our longings are met. Our identity, and everything we are, is found in Him.

I love the story of Nathanael, found in the Gospel of John, chapter 1. Nathanael, who became one of the 12 disciples of Jesus, was sitting under a fig tree, considering whether Jesus of Nazareth was truly the promised Messiah whom everyone was waiting for. His friend Philip, who was already a follower of Jesus, asked him to come and see for himself. He went to Jesus and was welcomed with the astonishing words:

*"Before Philip called you, when you were under the fig tree, I saw you"* (John 1:48).

Jesus revealed that He knew Nathanael before Nathanael met Him. The bottom line is: Jesus always finds us before we find Him!

It's interesting to listen to people share their testimonies of how they became a follower of Jesus. I will often hear someone share about the moment they "found" Jesus. But the reality is that none of us found Jesus before He had already found us. The parable of the lost sheep reminds us that without the shepherd, we would remain forever lost.

## IN THE IMAGE OF GOD

*"Or what woman, having ten silver coins, if she loses one coin, does not light a lamp, sweep the house, and search carefully until she finds it? And when she has found it, she calls her friends and neighbors together, saying, 'Rejoice with me, for I have found the piece which I lost!' Likewise, I say to you, there is joy in the presence of the angels of God over one sinner who repents"* (Luke 15:8-10).

The second story Jesus tells reveals the value of every single person in the eyes of God. A woman lost a silver coin, something of value to her. She made an effort to find the object, and rejoiced once it was found. Jesus likens this search and retrieval operation to a person repenting and turning to God. Just as the coin belonged to the woman, so we belong to God.

All the way back in the beginning of the scriptural narrative, we are told that God created humans in His image (Genesis 1:26). This is the first and probably most important thing to learn and know about us. We are created to reflect our Maker. Just as a coin often has an image on it, so we are image bearers. Sin has marred and tainted God's image in humans, but it is still there. If you have a coin with an almost erased image, it will still have the same value as one perfectly marked. We have not lost value in God's eyes. We still belong to Him. He is searching for His lost "image bearers," however faded and marred we have become.

When we become aware of how much He loves and values us, we will turn to Him. It is the goodness of God that leads us to repentance (Romans 2:4). Repentance is simply turning around. It has two dimensions. We turn away from sin, and we turn toward Jesus. True conversion is not just a behavioral improvement of our lives. It is rather a transformation, as we become aware of our own inability to change, and God's promise to do in us what we can't do for ourselves. Our focus is on Him. We start seeing in Him something better than what we had without Him.

At one time the Pharisees, the religious elite in the first century, came up to Jesus with a question designed to trick Him. They wanted to know whether or not Jesus thought they should pay taxes to Caesar (Matthew 22:17). In their minds they were pushing Jesus into a corner, believing that any answer was doomed to fail. There was a continual animosity between the Romans and the Jews, as the Jews were subjugated under Roman authority. If Jesus took the side of the Romans, He could easily be accused before the Jewish people. On the other hand, if Jesus showed any slight sign of rebellion against Rome, the Pharisees could use this to crush out His existence. Instead of giving a direct answer to their question, Jesus asked for a denarius, the coin of those days. In my mind's eye I can see Jesus lifting up the coin in front of the gathered crowd as He utters the words recorded in the Gospel of Matthew:

*"Whose image and inscription is this?"* The people respond with the correct answer: *"Caesar's"* (Matthew 22:20, 21).

The next words of Jesus, when closely considered, contain deep gospel truth:

*"And He said to them, 'Render therefore to Caesar the things that are Caesar's, and to God the things that are God's"* (verse 23).

You might be wondering where the gospel is in returning coins to Caesar. But pay close attention. Jesus made it plain that what is returned to Caesar is a coin that has his image on it. Immediately He added that we are to give to God the things that are God's. The question that begs to get asked here is: What belongs to God? The answer is simple: that which has His image! You and me! We are made in the image of God. God's stamp of love is all over us. It makes perfect sense that there is great rejoicing in heaven when we are found!

## CONTRACT OR COVENANT

In the third and final story of Jesus we are told about a father who had two sons. The younger one wanted an early inheritance, and claimed what was his. He left the family farm and journeyed to a faraway country, where he squandered all his belongings. Then times got tough, and a famine swept over the land. With nothing left, the young man found a job feeding pigs.

From a Jewish perspective, this occupation would have been considered the very bottom of the ladder. Jesus portrayed the dire and hopeless condition of the son who had once lived in abundance. He was now broke, hungry, lonely, and desperate. There must have been this moment of suspense as the listeners were wondering how this was all going to end. The next words of Jesus signified a turnaround in the story.

*"But when he came to himself, he said, 'How many of my father's hired servants have bread enough and to spare, and I perish with hunger! I will arise and go to my father, and will say to him, "Father, I have sinned against heaven and before you, and I am no longer worthy to be called your son. Make me like one of your hired servants"'"* (Luke 15:17-19).

*"But when he came to himself"*—it's as if a light bulb went on in his mind. He suddenly realized all the good that he had while he was with his father. He longed to go back, but believed that things would never be able to be the same. So he devised a plan. A strategy. A thought through script that would hopefully restore whatever could be restored. Notice that his prepared speech had two parts. First the acknowledgment of his actions (*"Father, I have sinned against heaven and before you"*). This was followed by a plan on how their relationship could be rearranged (*"I am no longer worthy to be called your son. Make me like one of your hired servants"*). He suggested a demotion from son to servant.

What he was really doing was seeking to enter a contract with his father. "I will do this if you do this." It accurately resembled the way many people relate to God. We want something from Him, and so we offer our services to earn whatever we want. We might not consciously be aware of this, but subconsciously it comes easy to relate to God based on a contract. All the while the God of the Scriptures is revealing that He is interested in entering a covenant with us.

There is a huge difference between a contract and a covenant. We will get back to this.

The prodigal son made the long journey back home, and Jesus brought another unexpected moment into the increasingly fascinating story.

*"But when he was still a great way off, his father saw him and had compassion, and ran and fell on his neck and kissed him"* (verse 20).

In those days it was very uncommon for the patriarch of the family to run. It just didn't happen. He was risking his respect and dignity for a wayward son. But something motivated this action. Love and compassion are always on the move. They act instead of reacting. They take the initiative. This is what we have seen again and again in these stories. God moves toward the sinner. Locked in the embrace of his father, the son tried to get out his speech but failed. Before he could offer his contract of becoming a servant instead of a son, his father confirmed his sonship. A celebratory feast was already in the making.

## LOST IN MORALITY AND RELIGIOSITY

This story is known as the parable of the lost son. However, as I mentioned in the beginning of this chapter, it is a parable about two lost sons. The story has two main scenes. The first scene is the story of the younger son, followed by the second scene depicting the older brother. Though at the outset these two men appeared very different, they also had striking similarities.

The older brother was the loyal son who continued to serve his father when his young sibling was gone. When he heard about the return of his brother and the feast that had been arranged, he refused to go in to celebrate. He was furious. His father left the party to reason with him. Take notice how the older brother strengthened his argument.

*"So he answered and said to his father, 'Lo, these many years I have been serving you; I never transgressed your commandment at any time; and yet you never gave me a young goat, that I might make merry with my friends. But as soon as this son of yours came, who has devoured your livelihood with harlots, you killed the fatted calf for him' "* (verses 29, 30).

The older son felt entitled and superior because of his years of service. He didn't waste his life in prodigal living, but he actually related to his father as a servant. In his mind the relationship was like a contract. "I have served, and therefore I deserve." Sounds familiar, right? This is what his younger brother attempted when he returned. Both sons had a distorted understanding of their relationship with their father. Both sons wanted the wealth and status of their father and tried to use him to get what they really wanted. One sought to achieve this by choosing to leave his father, while the other sought to accomplish this by staying with his father. One sought to gain control by breaking the rules, while the other sought to gain control by keeping the rules.

Jesus is showing us that both sons were lost and needed to

be found. This is the real eye-opening part of the story. Sin can often be covered up with self-righteousness. It is easy to see the sin in the younger brother, but Jesus turned the tables and showed the redemptive work in his life, while he left us wondering about the older brother. The parable is a cliff-hanger, as we never learn whether he went to the feast.

There are two types of lostness. You can avoid and resist God through immorality and irreligion, but you can perhaps less obviously avoid and resist him through morality and religion, when there is no personal relationship involved.

The older son listed his services in expectation of his father's blessings. His father replied by saying:

*"Son, you are always with me, and all that I have is yours"* (verse 31).

He was unfortunately not aware of the relationship he could have enjoyed all along. Sometimes we go through the forms of religion without being conscious of the blessings that are available.

## A FATHER'S HEART

Sadly, there are a lot of Christians walking in the footsteps of the older brother in this parable. We can't use God simply to get what we really want. Our desire must be to know Him and build a relationship with Him. We are to obey God, not because of what we get, but because of who He is. Remember that the parable has an open end, and God is pleading with us all to come to the feast.

The stories of Jesus in Luke 15 were an attempt to reveal the nature of Jesus' ministry on this earth. They were also designed to reveal the faulty thinking and acting of those who professed to follow God. The Pharisees complained about Jesus' approach to tax collectors and sinners. If they had listened carefully to the second half of the parable of the lost son(s), they would have recognized that Jesus was talking about them.

The older brother in the story was a striking representation of the Pharisees in the days of Jesus. They refused to rejoice over lost sinners who were found, as they deemed these individuals not worthy of God's favor and blessings. Jesus revealed in the parable the interest of the father for both the prodigal son and the older brother. In Jesus' earthly ministry He sought to reach the prodigals and the self-righteous. However, Jesus was met with increasing hostility by the religious leaders. This did not deter Him from reaching the outcasts and bringing them into His kingdom.

These parables reveal the enormous effort that was made to reach the lost. Ultimately it is God who finds us wherever we are. He meets us and draws us to Himself. Once the sheep was found, it was laid on the shoulders of the shepherd, and when the father saw his son in the distance, he ran and embraced him. There is a tenderness and love that is expressed. This, together with the joy that follows, reveals God's love for sinners who are lost. The gospel is the good news that we in Christ can move from being spiritually dead in our trespasses and sins to being alive in Him!

We have discovered something about the character of God. He is on the move! He is doing everything possible to find us wherever we are. Understanding this truth about God is preparing our soil, our lives, to receive His love. Only when we start to grasp our heavenly Father's love will we be able and willing to open up to His transformative work that He desires to do within each one of us. The more we behold His image, the more we will desire to be image bearers, reflecting His love to the world around us. In doing so, we are living out the purpose for which we are created.

So how can we avoid being in a contract with God? How can we make sure we are not repeating the older brother's arguments and missing out on the feast? What do we need to grasp in order to enter into the joy of God's covenant?

Stick around to find out!

# Chapter 3

# A TREASURE WORTH FINDING

The Parables of the Hidden Treasure and the Pearl of Great Price

Based on Matthew 13:44-46

I was born in New Zealand, though my parents came from the Netherlands. During my childhood I spent time in both countries, but for the past 20 years I have lived in the beautiful country of Norway. My wife is Norwegian, and I moved here when we got married.

Recently I had to take a Norwegian oral exam to officially become a Norwegian citizen. The oral exam was a mere formality, as I could already speak the language. As I drove to where the exam would take place, I sent up a prayer that if the opportunity would arise, I could share something about my faith. Norway is a very secular country, and religion is something that you don't share. You can talk about most other things, but this topic is just not really on the table. But it's usually possible to get in a sentence or two, especially when I am asked what I do for a living.

I arrived at the center and waited in the hallway together with a group of people that happened to schedule their exam the same day. We were randomly paired up and called in to the exam. I found myself sitting opposite a young Ukrainian woman, who had fled the war in her country and was now settling into a new country and learning a new language. The exam is set up in such a way that a moderator asks questions to the two of us, while two others in the room evaluate our skills.

She got the first question; the moderator asked her: "What things are most important for you in life? You have three minutes to answer."

I immediately thought to myself, *What a great question; I hope she asks me the same.* What happened next took me completely off guard. To say I was surprised would be an understatement. My new Ukrainian friend, whom I had never met before, spoke with confidence and conviction as she said: "What is most important for me is my faith in Jesus Christ!"

Not only did she make this bold statement, but she continued to elaborate and share why her faith in Jesus was so precious to her. She used her full three minutes to express what the gospel had meant for her when going through difficult times. Obviously she wasn't acquainted with the cultural unwritten "rule" of leaving these things out of discussions. I could hardly believe this was happening in a formal Norwegian exam.

The moderator listened carefully to her testimony. Thinking that we could now move on from this subject, she turned to me and asked me the same question! I was now emboldened and had no intention to merely include a sentence about my faith. My first words were: "I completely agree with her!"

I used my full three minutes to share what Jesus meant to me. I described how valuable the gospel was. It had become my ultimate treasure in life, and now I had the opportunity to hold up this treasure and show it to a group of random people at a Norwegian oral exam!

By this time the moderator and the two exam evaluators were wondering what was going on. Was this a setup? Where were the hidden cameras? The utter surprise written all over their faces was obvious. I am sure they had a lot to talk about once we left the room that day. For me it was something I call a divine appointment. When you live a life with God, you start to believe less and less in coincidence and more and more in providence. I believe God led both of us there that day and allowed us to lift up the treasure of the gospel in a secular place. Who knows what will result from this moment? Only eternity will tell.

One thing is sure. Once you have truly found the gospel

truth about the person Jesus, you will consider this your greatest treasure in life. There will be nothing more important than this. You will want to share Jesus with those around you.

## THE ULTIMATE TREASURE

Let us consider two of the shortest parables in the Bible, dealing with the discovery of this treasure.

*"Again, the kingdom of heaven is like treasure hidden in a field, which a man found and hid; and for joy over it he goes and sells all that he has and buys that field"* (Matthew 13:44).

Here is the first of the two parables. It's only one verse in the Bible. And yet this short parable is charged with profound insights into the gospel. It's probably good to start with a bit of historical background so we can more fully grasp what Jesus is depicting here.

In ancient times it was common for people to hide their treasures in the earth. Theft and robbery happened frequently, and they had no banks, so the earth became a secure place to hide valuable possessions. Sometimes the place of concealment was forgotten. The owner might die, or perhaps imprisonment or exile might separate him from his treasure. In Jesus' day it was not uncommon to discover coins, valuable objects, or even precious gold or silver in neglected fields. The man in the parable was not the owner of the land, but found the treasure hidden there. Whatever was found in the field belonged to the owner of that land.

Try imagining the scene that Jesus pictured in this short parable. The man may have been plowing and digging, and suddenly hit something with his tool. The sound he heard was different. This was not the regular stone or rock. It was something else. He then took a moment to remove some more soil. An object was now sticking out of the ground but was still stuck in the earth. His heart began to beat faster, and sweat appeared on his forehead and hands. He removed the dirt from the object, and it suddenly dawned on him that what he had found was of great value. He looked around to make sure no one was watching him. His eyes fastened again on the treasure, still lodged in the ground. Quickly he dug and loosened the treasure, lifting it toward him. It was heavy, but he could hold it in both his hands. For a moment he wondered if all of this was a dream he was about to wake up from. His mind raced as he tried to come to terms with what had just happened. This was going to change everything! He quickly realized that what he was holding in his hands was worth more than everything he owned. The value of the treasure surpassed all the man had in life. And yet he also understood that legally this treasure was not his, though he had found it. It belonged to the owner of the field. At that point he knew exactly what he needed to do. He carefully put the treasure back in the soil and covered it up, once again making sure no one had seen him.

It must have been hard for him to hold back his smile when he arrived home that day. But the secret needed to remain a secret for now. There was only one thing the man could think of. He needed to buy that field as soon as possible. But it was expensive, and he was poor. He started calculating his chances, and things looked dim. But perhaps he could just manage if he went all in and sold absolutely everything he owned. So he began the process. Perhaps we could liken it to a modern-day garage sale, except that the garage and house itself would have been included in the sale. Jesus made it clear in the parable that the man went and sold all that he had.

At this point, imagine what it must have looked like for his neighbors, friends, and family. They must have thought that he had absolutely lost his mind! Why in the world would you sell everything to buy a desolate, ugly, empty field? They see his possessions disappearing only for the prospect of a seemingly uninteresting piece of real estate. They have no idea that under the surface of this empty field is something extremely valuable. Can you imagine the day he finally purchased the field? His last penny was spent. He had nothing left! The only thing he now owned in life was a field. But then, to the utter surprise and amazement of the community, he suddenly became very wealthy. It all started with the discovery of a treasure.

The hidden treasure is a picture of the gospel of Jesus Christ. Once you come face-to-face with the good news about Jesus, you will see in Him a value that surpasses everything else. When you start pursuing Christ and the gospel, your priorities will start to change, and people around you will notice. They might think you are a bit crazy, just like the man in the parable. But you have seen something that others have not seen. Others may think that you are making a bad investment in life, but you know that obtaining the treasure of the gospel is worth everything. The essence of this parable is about discovering the value of the gospel in the person Jesus Christ, who is our ultimate treasure. It's about being willing to give up whatever is needed to be given up in order to have Jesus in our lives.

## FALSE EXPECTATIONS

The parable of the hidden treasure has another dimension that relates to the ancient Jewish nation and the ministry of Jesus in the first century. Erroneous traditions hindered the people from rightly understanding the prophecies about the coming Messiah. The religious leaders knew the text of Scripture by heart, but failed to recognize Jesus for who He was. They had false expectations. It's as if they possessed the field in the parable, and were in it, without having discovered the treasure right beneath them. They were waiting for a Messiah who could deliver them from the Romans and give them the honor and power they were looking for. It's interesting to note that the religious leaders in the first century wanted a new kingdom, but not the kind of kingdom Jesus introduced.

Have you ever heard about a person, before having met them, and created a picture of them in your mind, only to find out when actually meeting them that your perceived image did not fit reality? Suddenly the person you thought you knew looked and acted very different. This certainly happened more often when smartphones and social media were only a small part of our world.

Years ago I was invited to speak at a church in a country I had not been to before. The person I had planned the event with sent two of his young people from church to pick me up at the airport. They had never seen me and didn't know me at all. The only thing they had heard was that someone had said I was a missionary. They figured out that they could spot a missionary any day and needed no further instructions. Well, I didn't quite match their perceived image of me. I don't know exactly what they were looking for, but I didn't wear sandals, nor did I have a long beard. After quite a long wait at arrivals, I saw two young people glancing at me a few times. I approached them and introduced myself. The first thing they said was "You don't look like a missionary!" We had a good laugh.

The whole scene reminded me how easy it is to have a false expectation of someone. On a more serious note, this is exactly what happened to Jesus when He came into this world. People thought they knew what the Messiah would look like and what He would do. Jesus of Nazareth did not fit their perceived image. They were looking for a military figure who could free them from the Romans and establish an earthly kingdom. Instead, Jesus taught about a different kind of kingdom. A heavenly one!

Just as many people in the days of Jesus failed to recognize Him as the Messiah, so today many Christians go through the rhythms and traditions of church without having discovered for themselves the treasure and beauty of the gospel. Many people leave the church because they see only an "empty field." God has something far greater in store for us waiting to be discovered and enjoyed!

## COVENANT RELATIONSHIP

Do you remember our last parable from a chapter ago? We took a closer look at the story of the lost son and quickly discovered that his older brother was also lost and needed to be found. The younger son lived a prodigal life, but returned to his father, who graciously accepted him. A feast was prepared to celebrate the occasion, but the older brother did not want to join the party. He was angry and could not understand why his younger brother was being treated so well. After all, his younger brother did not deserve this honor, he felt. The older brother thought and acted in terms of a contract. In his mind his own relationship with his father was based on how much he had served, and therefore how much he deserved. All the while the father in the story was seeking a covenant relationship with him. He said, *"Son, you are always with me, and all that I have is yours"* (Luke 15:31).

The covenant theme runs through the whole narrative of Scripture. God is reassuring us again and again that although things have gone awfully wrong and sin has entered this world, He will conquer it and restore everything in the end. A covenant is an agreement between two parties. God seeks to enter a covenant with each of us, based on His promises. He lets us know that when we by faith receive Him, He will bring to pass all that He has promised He will do. In this covenant relationship it is all about His faithfulness in establishing His promises in our lives. We need to believe and trust that what He said will happen.

How is this connected to our parable about the discovered treasure? As we have seen, the treasure created joy in the man who found it. Jesus tells us that this joy led him to sell everything to buy the field. He was motivated by a joy for the treasure. In God's covenant relationship with us, we are to find a joy that surpasses everything else in life. We are to see in Christ and the gospel the greatest treasure we could ever possess.

The Christian life is more like a marathon than a sprint. For us to make it to the end, we need to be motivated by more than mere discipline. There needs to be a deep joy that is based on a profound appreciation for the gospel. We have found something that is priceless! For this treasure we are willing to give up everything. Our immense gratitude inspires us never to let go of Jesus, whatever the cost may be. We have entered the feast and tasted the goodness of God.

## SEARCHING FOR TRUTH

The parable of the hidden treasure is followed by the parable of the pearl of great price.

*"Again, the kingdom of heaven is like a merchant seeking beautiful pearls, who, when he had found one pearl of great price, went and sold all that he had and bought it"* (Matthew 13:45, 46).

Just as Christ is represented as the treasure in the first parable, so He is represented as the pearl of great price in the second parable. In Christ are *"hidden all the treasures of wisdom and knowledge"* (Colossians 2:3). All that can satisfy the needs and longings of the human soul, for this world and the world to come, is found in Him. Just as the pure white pearl is perfect without the influence of humans, so no one can improve the great and precious gift of God.

The merchant in the parable represents those who are seeking truth. According to the parable the merchant sells everything to buy the pearl. Salvation can of course not be purchased with money, so this transaction is speaking of something deeper.

The prophet Isaiah says:

*"Ho! Everyone who thirsts, come to the waters; and you who have no money, come, buy and eat. Yes, come, buy wine and milk without money and without price"* (Isaiah 55:1).

The only thing we give to Jesus in this transaction is our sin-polluted heart. In return we receive forgiveness, mercy, power, and all the riches of heaven in the person Jesus.

## HE GAVE EVERYTHING!

Ellen White provides a fascinating insight into this short parable:

"The parable of the merchantman seeking goodly pearls has a double significance: it applies not only to men as seeking the kingdom of heaven, but to Christ as seeking His lost inheritance.

Christ, the heavenly merchantman seeking goodly pearls, saw in lost humanity the pearl of price. In man, defiled and ruined by sin, He saw the possibilities of redemption. Hearts that have been the battleground of the conflict with Satan, and that have been rescued by the power of love, are more precious to the Redeemer than are those who have never fallen. God looked upon humanity, not as vile and worthless; He looked upon it in Christ, saw it as it might become through redeeming love. He collected all the riches of the universe, and laid them down in order to buy the pearl" (*Christ's Object Lessons*, p. 118).

Jesus sees in us a treasure, a pearl of great price, that is worth giving up everything to obtain. He gave up the glories of heaven, came down, and was born as a human being. He lived a life of service and gave His life on the cross to purchase you and me. If this is the price He was willing to pay for us, how much should we be willing to give and surrender to Him? The pearl of great price is worth everything, both for Jesus and for us.

## THE BEAUTY OF THE LORD

In Psalm 27 David writes:

*"One thing I have desired of the Lord, that will I seek: that I may dwell in the house of the Lord all the days of my life, to behold the beauty of the Lord, and to inquire in His temple"* (verse 4).

The parables of the hidden treasure and the pearl of great price are invitations to behold the beauty of the Lord. This beauty is found in the narrative of Scripture. When David saw the beauty of the Lord in the types and symbols of the sanctuary, he desired to learn more. He wanted to dwell in God's house and seek to understand God's plan of salvation more fully. The words of David indicate an ongoing pursuit of God. He had seen something, but he desired to see so much more. When we see the gospel for what it truly is, we will not be content with a mere glance at the story. We will desire to go deeper into the Scriptures, uncovering more and more treasure.

To experience the treasure found in God's Word, we need to

be born again. Jesus said to Nicodemus:

*"Most assuredly, I say to you, unless one is born again, he cannot see the kingdom of God"* (John 3:3).

We can grasp the kingdom of heaven only when our mind and heart have been awakened by God's Spirit. When Jesus taught in parables, some just heard stories, while others received principles and truths that led to change. Paul later wrote that *"the natural man does not receive the things of the Spirit of God, . . . because they are spiritually discerned"* (1 Corinthians 2:14). We need a spiritual mind to understand spiritual things.

The person Jesus cannot be detached from God's Word and His law. Once we truly discover the biblical Jesus, we will highly appreciate everything that points to Him. Discerning Jesus as our treasure leads us to have a high regard for God's revelation in the Scriptures. Without the Scriptures, we would not know Jesus. Too often Jesus is being separated from the teachings of the Bible, and a dichotomy is created between the two. But one does not exist without the other. We would not know about the character of Jesus without the gospel accounts. And even before the New Testament was written, Jesus said that the Scriptures testified of Him (John 5:39). He was referring to the Old Testament scriptures. The prophets had predicted in types, symbols, and prophecies that a Messiah would come, and He came! The entire Bible leads us to Him.

The Bible describes a universe in which there are good and evil forces at war with each other. While God reveals to us His Word, there is an enemy who is doing everything to hinder us from pursuing this treasure. In our next chapter we will explore a parable that will unfold for us this great controversy of which we are all part. We are truly caught in the crossfire.

But there is good news! Jesus has gained a decisive victory over the enemy that can impact each of us.

Chapter 4

# CAUGHT IN THE CROSSFIRE

The Parable of the Wheat and the Tares

Based on Matthew 13:24-30

During World War II Germany invaded Norway, and in the early stages of the occupation there was fighting taking place in different parts of the country. My wife's grandfather, named Gunnar, told us about an experience he had as a young man during that time. He attended a home church gathering, and after singing and praying, the group began their Bible study. They had barely finished the service when they heard sudden gunshots. A fighter plane had targeted the house they were in, and shortly after, gunshots were exchanged between the approaching German army and the Norwegian resistance fighters. As the battle intensified, the small band of Adventist Christians quickly made their way to safety. After much prayer and waiting, huddled in the basement, they made their way back to the living room of the house. To his utter surprise and shock, Gunnar noticed that several bullets had pierced the coat he had left behind! You can imagine how grateful he was for God's protection! He was literally caught in the crossfire, and yet God had preserved his life.

## A GOOD GOD AND A BAD WORLD

Jesus told a parable about how we are all caught up in a larger battle between good and evil. The parable of the wheat and the tares gives us an insight into the war that is raging in the universe.

*"Another parable He put forth to them, saying: 'The kingdom of heaven is like a man who sowed good seed in his field; but while men*

*slept, his enemy came and sowed tares among the wheat and went his way. But when the grain had sprouted and produced a crop, then the tares also appeared. So the servants of the owner came and said to him, "Sir, did you not sow good seed in your field? How then does it have tares?" He said to them, "An enemy has done this." The servants said to him, "Do you want us then to go and gather them up?" But he said, "No, lest while you gather up the tares you also uproot the wheat with them. Let both grow together until the harvest, and at the time of harvest I will say to the reapers, 'First gather together the tares and bind them in bundles to burn them, but gather the wheat into my barn'"'"*(Matthew 13:24-30).

Jesus had been teaching all day, and multitudes had flocked to listen to Him. The parable of the wheat and the tares was one of the many parables Jesus shared that day. As the sun began to set on the horizon, Jesus left the multitude and entered a house. His disciples were with Him, and there was so much for them to process. They had the privilege of not just hearing the teachings of Jesus together with the rest of the people, but being part of the inner circle. This meant they could probe into the deeper meaning of Jesus' stories. One parable stuck out among the others. One story had been swirling in their mind for much of the day. They are desperate to know more.

*"And His disciples came to Him, saying, 'Explain to us the parable of the tares of the field' "* (verse 36).

The parable was not just about tares (weeds). This act of the enemy perplexed them, and they were curious what this meant. The age-old question about where evil comes from has been on the minds of millions throughout the centuries. The question comes in different shapes and forms, but ultimately wrestles with the fact that we encounter things in this life that we sense are not supposed to be this way.

Many struggle with what seems to be a dichotomy: a God of love and a world of suffering.

The question is asked: If there is a God of love, why is there so much suffering in the world?

Notice that the question itself immediately reveals something. We put value on people and creation. People were not meant to suffer, and the world was not meant to be like it is. In a world of "survival of the fittest," this question makes no sense. As a matter of fact, some must suffer for others to succeed. Some foremost atheists make the bold claim that there is no such thing as evil, and that we are all merely dancing to our DNA. Why would they go to such lengths as to deny the very existence of evil? Isn't it obvious that there is such a thing as evil that is causing suffering in our world? However, the denial of evil is a thought through position that fits in the overall atheistic worldview. Because evil implies a moral responsibility. After all, evil is most often attributed to the actions of people. Follow the logic here. If there is such a thing as the existence of evil, there must also be the existence of good, or else we would not be able to distinguish the two. If there is such a thing as good and evil, we need a moral standard to know the difference. If there is a moral standard, it must come from somewhere. We would need a moral standard giver who is beyond us, and the idea of a God is suddenly on the table!

It does not make sense to talk about good and evil in an atheistic worldview, where there is no framework for any moral norm. I am not saying that atheists themselves are not motivated by moral virtues. It's just that it does not theoretically match with their perception of reality. But the fact that people from all different worldviews, including atheists, are asking the same questions regarding the existence of evil is significant. It's as though we intuitively know that this is not the way things were meant to be. Something has gone wrong, and this is exactly what the parable of Jesus is getting at.

## THE ORIGIN OF EVIL

The Bible reveals how people throughout the centuries have navigated through pain and struggle. Such books as Job and the Psalms display real people crying out to God for answers. The solution is not simplistic. Remember that the tares were sown at night. There is something mysterious and hidden about the origin of evil, but the Bible does reveal enough for us to understand the big picture. The parable of the wheat and the tares gives us a framework of the battle between good and evil.

When Jesus explained the parable, He identified the devil as the enemy (verse 39). There are several other portions of Scripture that describe this enemy as an exalted angel named Lucifer, who rebelled against his maker (Isaiah 14:12-14; Ezekiel 28:12-15; Revelation 12:4, 7-9). Lucifer, along with a third of the angels who sided with him in his rebellion, were removed from heaven. The big question that rises is why God created Lucifer, who brought sin into the universe. The answer lies in the very character of God.

The Bible tells us that "God is love" (1 John 4:8). For love to be real, it must give freedom of choice. God did not want the love of programmed angels and humans. None of us are moved by a computer that is programmed to say: "I love you." A volitionary will must be in the picture here. Love requires freedom, but freedom involves risk. This risk exists only because humans are created with a moral responsibility. We can choose to love or not to love.

These concepts are connected and are central to the great controversy story. The field in the parable is a picture of the world (Matthew 13:38). We live in a world with "wheat and tares." In this world there is a great potential for good and a great potential for evil. The world looks like a battlefield because it is one. We often wonder why suffering seems to continue for so long.

In the parable the owner of the field said concerning the wheat and the tares:

*"Let both grow together until the harvest"* (verse 30).

The development and fruition of evil needs to be seen in the universe for it to be fully exposed for what it truly is.

The harvest, *"the end of the age"* (verse 39), will eventually come. Final judgement takes place only when all have seen the outcome of evil. The parable describes two groups of people:

*"The good seeds are the sons of the kingdom, but the tares are the sons of the wicked one"* (verse 38).

All people make decisions throughout life that determine on which side they stand in this battle between good and evil.

## THE SON OF MAN

In the parable the man sowing the good seed is identified as the *"Son of Man"* (verse 37). Jesus often used this description when pointing to Himself.

The Son of Man is also presented as the one separating the wheat from the tares when the time of harvest finally comes:

*"The Son of Man will send out His angels, and they will gather out of His kingdom all things that offend, and those who practice lawlessness, and will cast them into the furnace of fire. There will be wailing and gnashing of teeth. Then the righteous will shine forth as the sun in the kingdom of their Father. He who has ears to hear, let him hear!"* (verses 41-43).

Jesus sows the good seed and harvests the good wheat. He is actively involved in preparing people to inherit His everlasting kingdom. Jesus comes beside us in our suffering. He became one of us and knows what we are going through. In a world in which evil exists, He reveals His goodness. There are many examples of this throughout Scripture.

David wrote about his own experience of God's goodness in times of difficulty. In his most famous psalm he displays the goodness of God even in the dark valleys of life. The God described in this psalm is the same God who came into this world and walked among us. David writes:

*"The Lord is my shepherd; I shall not want. He makes me lie down in green pastures; He leads me beside the still waters. He restores my soul; He leads me in the paths of righteousness for His name's sake. Yea, though I walk through the valley of the shadow of death, I will fear no evil; for You are with me; Your rod and Your staff, they comfort me"* (Psalm 23:1-4).

In a world with dark valleys, we have someone who is by our side. Jesus is called Immanuel, meaning "God with us." David discerned God's protection even when he was a fugitive, and his life was endangered. His focus was on the goodness of God.

*"Surely goodness and mercy shall follow me all the days of my life; and I will dwell in the house of the Lord forever"* (verse 6).

It's the goodness of God that leads us to repentance (Romans 2:4). His goodness allows us to grow spiritually. Jesus reveals in the parable that we belong to God, and that He is doing all in His power to prepare us for His eternal kingdom.

## THE GREATEST SACRIFICE

Bobby Fischer is considered one of the greatest chess players in the history of chess. He was still very young when he became world-famous. On October 17, 1956, Bobby played against a seasoned champion by the name of Donald Byrne. Bobby was only 13 years old at the time, while Donald was in his early 50s. This match went down into history as the game of the century. From the outset there was something novel about a child making it so far in the world of chess. Commentators were following every move as they studied the progression of both players. A drastic moment occurred when Bobby came to his now-famous seventeenth move. He moved his queen so it could be taken. Everyone thought young Bobby had lost the game. The commentators were quick to point out this terrible mistake. What could you expect from a 13-year-old, anyway? He had done well to make it so far, but obviously needed a lot more experience. Donald, as expected, took the queen. However, over the course of the next 20-some moves, he lost the game! Bobby, instead of making a terrible mistake, had made a thought-through strategic move! He gave his queen away, believing that this move would set in motion a sequence of moves that would lead him to win the game. And he was right! Bobby Fischer was able to see the whole game in front of him and considered the losing of his queen ultimately an advantage. This famous move is referred to as the greatest sacrifice in the game of chess!

The gospel is a story of an unexpected victory. It also involves an unexpected sacrifice. None of the Jewish religious leaders expected the Messiah to sacrifice his life. They were waiting for a Messiah figure who would overthrow their enemies and establish a glorious earthly kingdom. Not even the closest disciples of Jesus understood His mission. When Jesus died on the cross, it was seen as an utter defeat. No victory was discerned on that dark day. But with hindsight we look back on the moment Jesus cried out His last words, *"It is finished"* (John 19:30), and we now know these words meant victory. What was finished? The perfect plan of God had been accomplished! Jesus, who had been one with God, had laid off His divinity and come down to this earth. He had become the *"Son of Man,"* as one of us. All His life was marked by purity and truth. He who knew no sin became sin for us (2 Corinthians 5:21). All the sin, evil, and transgression of the entire human race was laid on Him. The consequence of sin is death, and on the cross Jesus died for you and me. He takes our place to grant us the gift of eternal life (Romans 6:23).

Hundreds of years before, the prophet Isaiah had predicted what would happen to the Messiah. In one of the most gripping chapters in Scripture we have an accurate description of the rejection of Jesus, but also what He accomplished on the cross for us. These words of Isaiah are like a biography of Jesus, only written long before He was born!

*"Who has believed our report?*
*And to whom has the arm of the Lord been revealed?*
*For He shall grow up before Him as a tender plant,*
*And as a root out of dry ground.*
*He has no form or comeliness;*
*And when we see Him,*
*There is no beauty that we should desire Him.*
*He is despised and rejected by men,*
*A Man of sorrows and acquainted with grief.*

*And we hid, as it were, our faces from Him;*
*He was despised, and we did not esteem Him.*
*Surely He has borne our griefs*
*And carried our sorrows;*
*Yet we esteemed Him stricken,*
*Smitten by God, and afflicted.*
*But He was wounded for our transgressions,*
*He was bruised for our iniquities;*
*The chastisement for our peace was upon Him,*
*And by His stripes we are healed.*
*All we like sheep have gone astray;*
*We have turned, every one, to his own way;*
*And the Lord has laid on Him the iniquity of us all.*
*He was oppressed and He was afflicted,*
*Yet He opened not His mouth;*
*He was led as a lamb to the slaughter,*
*And as a sheep before its shearers is silent,*
*So He opened not His mouth.*
*He was taken from prison and from judgment,*
*And who will declare His generation?*
*For He was cut off from the land of the living;*
*For the transgressions of My people He was stricken.*
*And they made His grave with the wicked—*
*But with the rich at His death,*
*Because He had done no violence,*
*Nor was any deceit in His mouth"* (Isaiah 53:1-9).

The unexpected sacrifice of Jesus had been prophesied. The words of Isaiah came to pass when Jesus was crucified. People looked at the scene, but saw only defeat.

However, Jesus Himself knew that His sacrifice on the cross would lead to a victory over the enemy. Listen to His words recorded in the Gospel of John:

*"'Now is the judgment of this world; now the ruler of this world will be cast out. And I, if I am lifted up from the earth, will draw all peoples to Myself.' This He said, signifying by what death He*

*would die"* (John 12:31–33).

Jesus knew that His death would result in the enemy being *"cast out."* People would be drawn to Him. This has definitely happened! People all over the world recognize the death and resurrection of Jesus as an absolute victory over evil, sin, and death.

## A CONQUERED ENEMY

The phrase *"cast out"* is used by John in another book he wrote. At the end of the Bible we have the book of Revelation. Take notice how John portrays the enemy's defeat and desperation.

*"So the great dragon was cast out, that serpent of old, called the Devil and Satan, who deceives the whole world; he was cast to the earth, and his angels were cast out with him. Then I heard a loud voice saying in heaven, 'Now salvation, and strength, and the kingdom of our God, and the power of His Christ have come, for the accuser of our brethren, who accused them before our God day and night, has been cast down. And they overcame him by the blood of the Lamb and by the word of their testimony, and they did not love their lives to the death. Therefore rejoice, O heavens, and you who dwell in them! Woe to the inhabitants of the earth and the sea! For the devil has come down to you, having great wrath, because he knows that he has a short time' "* (Revelation 12:9–12).

We are living about 2,000 years after the death and resurrection of Jesus. His death and victory are a fact of history. The enemy's arguments and lies have been exposed and dismantled. They were cast down at the cross! Jesus revealed God's love through His life and sacrifice. The enemy could no longer refute what had now been openly displayed in front of the whole universe. No wonder Paul penned these words when contemplating what the cross of Jesus had accomplished:

*"Having disarmed principalities and powers, He made a public spectacle of them, triumphing over them in it"* (Colossians 2:15).

What a conquest! But this absolute victory is seen only when the gospel is seen. It's only when we start understanding the significance of the death and resurrection of Jesus that we accept the victory that has been accomplished for us.

Though a mighty victory has been won on the cross, the great controversy between good and evil has not ended yet. A defeated foe is still spreading his lies. We are still in the field of the parable, where we continually behold the wheat and the tares. People are responding either to the truth of the gospel or to the lies of the enemy. This is producing the sons of the kingdom and the sons of the wicked one (Matthew 13:38). We are all caught in the crossfire of this ongoing battle and there is no middle ground.

## THE CORE OF THE CONFLICT

Jesus tells us in the explanation of the parable, that those who follow the enemy practice lawlessness (Matthew 13:41). This battle between good and evil revolves around the gospel, but also the law of God. Ever since the beginning of the great controversy, Lucifer has made war on God's law. This continues to be at the epicenter of the conflict.

In our previous parable we looked at the gospel of Jesus as a treasure we are to discover. This treasure includes the law of God, revealed in the Ten Commandments. Jesus affirmed and exemplified in His life the value and importance of the law. When we take a closer look at the Ten Commandments, we see how God has designed a beautiful covenant plan. The psalmist David recognized this when he cried out:

*"Oh, how I love Your law! It is my meditation all the day"* (Psalm 119:97).

He saw in God's commandments a treasure of great value. Once we look at God's Ten Commandments through the lens of the gospel, we see how God values us. He assures us that we are His.

The first commandment is like a marriage vow:

*"I am the Lord your God, who brought you out of the land of*

*Egypt, out of the house of bondage. You shall have no other gods before Me"* (Exodus 20:2, 3).

God is promising us that He is all we need. He will be everything to us! He has set us free from the bondage of sin, and we belong to Him.

If we relate to God with a contract mindset, the Ten Commandments will appear like 10 restrictions on our lives. We will seek to keep them dutifully to gain a reward, while lacking the deep joy God wants to give us. Unfortunately, this approach has led many to either fall into despair or, like the Pharisees, think they are better than everyone else. But once we experience a paradigm shift, we view God's law as a treasure. His commandments become promises of who He is and what He wants to do in our lives.

The first commandment, or promise, reminds us that we belong to Him.

This is followed by the assurance that we don't have to wonder what He is like. We don't need to make any carved images of Him (verse 4). The promise is that He will reveal Himself to us. And when He does so, we will understand better what He is like.

The third commandment is about taking the name of God in vain (verse 7). In Scripture the name of God is often synonymous with His character. Moses once asked God to reveal His glory, and God passed by before him, declaring His name. His name was a description of His character, the kind of God He is. It makes sense that once we get to know God, we will no longer be prone to misrepresent Him. This is another promise!

The fourth commandment is a promise that God wants to spend time with us (verses 8-11). Every parent will know that the greatest gift you can give to your children is time. By giving your time, you are giving of yourself. God is pursuing a relationship with us. In the fourth commandment He reminds us that He created the world in six days and set aside the seventh day (Saturday). The seventh day has been marked as sacred time.

We remember who created us and to whom we belong. The Sabbath is a gift to all humanity!

Every commandment is a promise, revealing something about God and something He wants to accomplish in us.

The tenth and last command says: *"You shall not covet"* (verse 17).

It's again a promise! Because once Jesus becomes our treasure, and His law becomes our delight, we will be so satisfied and fulfilled in Him that we will not need anything else to fill the void. He has already filled it by giving us a purpose and a value that this world cannot give. Without Him we will continue to covet the things of this world to fill the space that only He can fill. But once we have discovered the treasure of the gospel and the beauty of His law, all worldly treasures will appear dim in comparison.

Though we are caught in the crossfire of a battle between good and evil, we can find victory in Christ. He has promised that in the new covenant He will write His commandments in our hearts.

*" 'This is the covenant that I will make with them after those days, says the Lord: I will put My laws into their hearts, and in their minds I will write them,' then He adds, 'Their sins and their lawless deeds I will remember no more' "* (Hebrews 10:16, 17).

Wow! What a promise! What a victory!

In our next chapter we will take a closer look at a parable that reveals how we can tap into God's power in order to resist the enemy and grow in faith.

# Chapter 5

# NEVER GIVE UP!

## The Parable of the Friend at Midnight

## Based on Luke 11:5-13

A few years ago I was preaching in Oslo, the capital of Norway. After the service my family and I strolled from the church toward the palace of the king, which is in the center of the city. We walked through the palace gardens and watched the king's guards march in front of the gates. Suddenly my then 5-year-old son turned to me and said, "I want to visit the king! I want to go into the palace and see the king!" I had to explain to him that it does not quite work like that. No one can just drop in. There are secretaries, procedures, gates, and a whole lot more that I probably don't even know about. Earthly kings are available only to a chosen few. But that day I told my son about another King, who is always available. Jesus is our ultimate king, and He has told us that we can come to Him whenever. It does not matter where we are, as we can instantly connect with Him through prayer. He is waiting to hear from us.

But often we don't experience immediate answers to our prayers, and sometimes we wonder if God hears us at all. What are we to do in those moments?

## A RELATIONAL AND ACCESSIBLE GOD

In this chapter we will look at the parable of the persistent friend. Through this story Jesus is encouraging us not to give up when bringing our requests to God. It is through persistent prayer we reveal that we believe His promises to be true, even when they are not answered immediately in the way we expect. Prayer strengthens our faith as we continue to press closer to God.

Before we take a closer look at the actual parable, it is important to note the setting it is given in. The Gospel of Luke makes it clear that the parable of the persistent friend follows immediately after the prayer that Jesus exemplified before His disciples. The prayer of Jesus, known as the Lord's Prayer, reveals that God is approachable and accessible to every seeker. The parable builds on this idea.

In the prayer we are invited to address God as our Father. Ellen White writes:

"The very first step in approaching God is to know and believe the love that He has to us (1 John 4:16); for it is through the drawing of His love that we are led to come to Him" (*Thoughts From the Mount of Blessing*, pp. 104, 105).

We approach God when we understand His profound love toward us. This draws us to come to Him in prayer.

The first words in the Lord's Prayer are *"Our Father in heaven"* (Luke 11:2). This immediately reveals the relationship God wants with us. His love as our heavenly Father draws us to Him.

We are invited to address a personal being in a specific place. God is of course not limited to one place, as we learn in Scripture that He is omnipresent (everywhere) and omniscient (all knowing). However, there are many new forms of spirituality rising, teaching that God is a force to be found in the objects of nature, as well as inside each of us. This teaching, often referred to as pantheism, leads people to seek God within themselves, but this is not how Jesus taught us to pray.

We are told that the heart is wicked and *"deceitful above all things"* (Jeremiah 17:9). This means that we cannot trust our inner being, but need to surrender our hearts to a power outside of us. This is so important, as it is our access point. The transformational power in prayer comes from outside of us as we connect with our heavenly Father. The rest of the Lord's Prayer flows out of this. His will can be done, His name (character) can be seen, His kingdom can come (Luke 11:2) when we first seek His person, power, and presence. We come to our heavenly Father stained by sin. Our sin is a result of our following our own will. Now we seek Him and plead for forgiveness. Our sins are forgiven, and His will is wrought in our lives. His kingdom has come!

## PERSEVERANCE IN PRAYER

With the backdrop of a relational accessible heavenly Father, we are launched into the parable of the persistent friend. Through the parable Jesus urges us to seek God and be persistent in prayer.

*"And He said to them, 'Which of you shall have a friend, and go to him at midnight and say to him, "Friend, lend me three loaves; for a friend of mine has come to me on his journey, and I have nothing to set before him"; and he will answer from within and say, "Do not trouble me; the door is now shut, and my children are with me in bed; I cannot rise and give to you"? I say to you, though he will not rise and give to him because he is his friend, yet because of his persistence he will rise and give him as many as he needs.*

*"'So I say to you, ask, and it will be given to you; seek, and you will find; knock, and it will be opened to you. For everyone who asks receives, and he who seeks finds, and to him who knocks it will be opened. If a son asks for bread from any father among you, will he give him a stone? Or if he asks for a fish, will he give him a serpent instead of a fish? Or if he asks for an egg, will he offer him a scorpion? If you then, being evil, know how to give good gifts to your children, how much more will your heavenly Father give the Holy Spirit to those who ask Him!' "* (Luke 11:5-13).

A little historic background for the parable will help us grasp the scene. In first-century Palestine hospitality was not just an option but a must. When the man in the parable got visitors, it was crucial for him to be able to provide a meal for them. Meals were considered a social event, to gather and unite people together. Food was scarce, and people had to work hard to provide for the daily needs of their families. The man without bread, described in the parable, had a dilemma. Either he was going to be a poor host or bother his neighbor in the middle of the night. He considered that disturbing his friend was the better option. This was not just a little inconvenient. He really bothered his neighbor!

Most houses in those days were simply one-room houses. The whole family would often sleep together in one room. Security was important, so the door was bolted after the family had retired for the night. The knocking on the door would most likely wake the whole family. It's one thing to wake up an adult; it's something else to wake up a 1-year-old! No wonder he started his plea with the word "friend." Jesus made the point that though it was highly inconvenient for the neighbor, he would still provide bread because of the persistence of the man. He just didn't want to be bothered anymore.

A surface look at this parable could cause us to come to a very faulty conclusion of what Jesus was teaching here. Often we try to find our role and God's role in the parables so that we can draw a comparison on how He relates to us and how we are to relate to Him. If we would make a comparison in this instance, we would be the man who needed the bread, and God was obviously the one who provided the bread. This is what the Lord's Prayer focused on: *"Give us day by day our daily bread"* (Luke 11:3). But this would mean that we are bothering God when we come to Him in prayer. How would you feel being the man having to knock on the door in the middle of the night, asking for bread? Is this how we should feel when approaching God? Am I just bothering Him with the little details of my life? After all, He has an entire universe to run! But perhaps if I ask long enough, He will give me what I need so I stop bothering Him. Is this the picture we should get? I am glad it isn't!

## HOW MUCH MORE

The whole story falls into place once we understand that the parable is not a comparison but a contrast. We are still the one asking, but if even the woken-up neighbor eventually gives the bread, *"how much more"* will not God give to those who ask Him! The key phrase here is *"how much more."*

*"If you then, being evil, know how to give good gifts to your children, how much more will your heavenly Father give the* Holy Spirt to

*those who ask Him!"* (Luke 11:13).

I have been writing this book from my home office, and every once in a while my sons, ages 9 and 7, will wander in. A few times they have shown me a drawing they had been working on. On a few occasions they had a question they needed my help with or an issue that needed to get solved. Other times they were simply curious what I was doing and were just looking for some contact. At these moments I would stop writing and give them my attention. My children live in their own world of little joys and little sorrows. I want them to be able to have access to me so I can share in their experiences. Even the seemingly insignificant things are significant to me, simply because they are my children.

How confident are you in approaching your heavenly Father? He is accessible, and you can go to Him with the big as well as the small things of life. He is waiting to receive us. Jesus wants us to put ourselves in the shoes of the man needing bread. If he is bold and shameless enough to ask his neighbor for bread in the middle of the night, how much more will your heavenly Father give to those who come to Him and are persistent in seeking for heavenly gifts. Don't give up when seeking God in prayer. Keep knocking! God wants us to "bother" Him with the things that occupy our lives.

## GOD'S PRESENCE

In the Old Testament, God revealed His presence through the sanctuary and its services. This was at first a tent structure in the wilderness after the Hebrews had left Egypt. Later they built a permanent temple in Jerusalem. The sanctuary was a place of worship and prayer. Much of the book of Exodus describes in detailed manner the building of the sanctuary. The last verses of Exodus are fascinating as we come to the moment the wilderness sanctuary was inaugurated. God literally showed up!

*"Then the cloud covered the tabernacle of meeting, and the glory of the Lord filled the tabernacle. And Moses was not able to enter the tabernacle of meeting, because the cloud rested above it, and the glory of*

*the Lord filled the tabernacle"* (Exodus 40:34, 35).

I personally don't know of any church opening ceremony that has experienced the like of this! Can you imagine seeing God's glory in such a tangible way? This was not the only time this happened. Fast-forward the story a few hundred years. The Hebrews are now living in the promised land of Canaan and have built a temple in Jerusalem. They are gathered with King Solomon to inaugurate the temple. What do you think they are expecting? The presence of God manifested in a cloud of glory! And guess what: it happens again!

*"And it came to pass, when the priests came out of the holy place, that the cloud filled the house of the Lord, so that the priests could not continue ministering because of the cloud; for the glory of the Lord filled the house of the Lord"* (1 Kings 8:10, 11).

Can you imagine the excitement? Shouts of joy must have filled the air! God is with us!

Again, we fast-forward the story. Hundreds of years go by, and Israel loses sight of God. God still wants to be with them, but they no longer want to be with Him. Sin, corruption, and oppression fill the land; God's protection is slowly removed, and the northern and southern kingdoms are eventually overpowered by neighboring nations. Judah is exiled into captivity for 70 years in Babylon. After the 70 years the Persian king releases the Jews and allows them to return to Jerusalem, where they start rebuilding the Temple. As stone is laid upon stone, what do you think the people are expecting? The presence of God to again fill the temple!

Inauguration day arrives, and the people are all gathered. The second temple was raised in the midst of ruins and certainly did not look as impressive as Solomon's temple. But if they could only know that God was still with them! However, this time no glorious cloud descended from heaven. There was no physical manifestation of God's presence. In the silence they waited for a sign, but no apparent sign came.

However, this didn't mean that God was not with them. In their midst stood a prophet, whom God had sent to them at this very time. His name was Haggai, and he wrote a book that we have in our Bibles. God used Haggai as His spokesperson and gave a promise to His people.

"'Who is left among you who saw this temple in its former glory? And how do you see it now? In comparison with it, is this not in your eyes as nothing? Yet now be strong, Zerubbabel,' says the Lord; 'and be strong, Joshua, son of Jehozadak, the high priest; and be strong, all you people of the land,' says the Lord, 'and work; for I am with you,' says the Lord of hosts. 'According to the word that I covenanted with you when you came out of Egypt, so My Spirit remains among you; do not fear!' " (Haggai 2:3-5).

God assures His people that He is still with them. This was a promise that they were to hold on to. Though there was no physical manifestation of glory, there was a precious promise given through a prophet sent by God. And the words of this prophet predicted what was going to happen in the future.

"For thus says the Lord of hosts: 'Once more (it is a little while) I will shake heaven and earth, the sea and dry land; and I will shake all nations, and they shall come to the Desire of All Nations, and I will fill this temple with glory,' says the Lord of hosts. 'The silver is Mine, and the gold is Mine,' says the Lord of hosts. 'The glory of this latter temple shall be greater than the former,' says the Lord of hosts. 'And in this place I will give peace,' says the Lord of hosts" (verses 6-9).

Incredible! Ultimately the second temple would be more glorious than the first. Why? Jesus, the Desire of Ages, would walk in that temple! Hundreds of years later the promise would be fulfilled. Jesus, at the age of 12, joined His parents going to Jerusalem to celebrate the Passover. He walked into the temple, and glory filled the house!

Only this time, no one noticed it.

God had never been more approachable. Here He was in the flesh. One of the names of Jesus is Immanuel, meaning God with us! And though God was so near, the people did not recognize Him and were still waiting for a sign.

## HIS PROMISES WILL NOT FAIL

Have you ever wondered if God is with you? Perhaps you are going through a season of life in which there is seemingly no external sign of His presence. Maybe you sometimes feel you cannot approach Him. At times we live in expectancy for some sign of God's favor in our life, and there seems to be none. Perhaps it's the ordinary flow of life that eclipses you from seeing Him. You want an experience with God, but you feel your prayers are bouncing back on you. What you need to know is that God is with you on the ordinary Monday morning! What we need to remember is that we have precious promises in God's Word that are always available to us. When we don't see the sign we are waiting for, we can cling to the promises that never fail.

While we are persistent in prayer, we can pray the promises of God back to Him. Here are some examples of promises you can pray.

*Dear heavenly Father: You said that "You will keep him in perfect peace whose mind is stayed on You"* (Isaiah 26:3).

*You said that I can "lie down in peace, and sleep" and that You will keep me safe* (Psalm 4:8).

*You said that You would take away my fear and give me "love" and "a sound mind"* (2 Timothy 1:7).

*You said that when You begin "a good work" in someone, You "will complete it"* (Philippians 1:6).

*You said that we should not be weary in well doing, for" in due season we shall reap"* (Galatians 6:9).

*You said that You would wake me up in the morning and give me the right words to speak to those who are weary* (Isaiah 50:4).

*You said Your Word would not return void to You, but accomplish that in which you are pleased* (Isaiah 55:11).

*You have said that all our children will be taught by You, and great will be their peace* (Isaiah 54:13).

*Thank You, God! You said that when I don't know how to pray, Your Spirit will intercede for me* (Romans 8:26).

You don't have to feel super-spiritual to pray these kinds of prayers. All you need is faith that God hears you. Our feelings will often fluctuate in life, but our faith can remain constant.

## FAITH AND FEELING

Sadly, many don't understand the difference between faith and feeling. Ellen White describes this well:

"Feeling and faith are as distinct from each other as the east is from the west. Faith is not dependent on feeling. Daily we should dedicate ourselves to God, and believe that Christ understands and accepts the sacrifice, without examining ourselves to see if we have that degree of feeling that we think should correspond with our faith. Have we not the assurance that our heavenly Father is more willing to give the Holy Spirit to them that ask Him in faith than parents are to give good gifts to their children? We should go forward as if to every prayer that we send to the throne of God we heard the response from the One whose promises never fail. Even when depressed by sadness it is our privilege to make melody in our hearts to God. When we do this the mists and clouds will be rolled back and we will pass from the shadow and darkness into the clear sunshine of His presence" (*Our High Calling*, p. 120).

Our feelings will at times seek to lead us to believe that God is distant. Our feelings may even suggest that God does not hear our prayers. The apostle Paul admonishes us to *"fight the good fight of faith"* (1 Timothy 6:12). In these moments we need to be persistent as we take hold of God's precious promises. Never give up!

Because of what Jesus has done, and the victory He has gained, all God's promises are now ours. The apostle Paul puts it this way:

*"For all the promises of God in Him are Yes, and in Him Amen, to the glory of God through us"* (2 Corinthians 1:20).

I often remind myself what the Christian faith rests on. It's the objective truth of a historical event. I can't change what happened 2,000 years ago. Christ came into this world and was incarnated as the *"Son of Man."* He lived a perfect life and died for my sins. On the first day of the week He rose from the grave victoriously. He ascended back to heaven, where He now prays for me as my high priest in the heavenly sanctuary. This is all true, whether I feel it or not. I can believe this by faith, even in those moments my subjective feelings seek to suggest something else. A faith in what I know to be true will help me to fight feelings of doubt and distrust. As we persist in prayer, claiming God's promises by faith, we can enter the sunshine of His presence. Don't give up when clouds surround you. Claim the promises that are yours in Christ. Because of Jesus, we can approach God's throne with great courage.

*"Seeing then that we have a great High Priest who has passed through the heavens, Jesus the Son of God, let us hold fast our confession. For we do not have a High Priest who cannot sympathize with our weaknesses, but was in all points tempted as we are, yet without sin. Let us therefore come boldly to the throne of grace, that we may obtain mercy and find grace to help in time of need"* (Hebrews 4:14–16).

His throne is called a throne of grace! We can come to the One who shows us mercy!

I am reminded of the Old Testament story of Queen Esther, who in a providential way became queen in Persia. When the Jews were threatened to be annihilated through an evil scheme, she stood up for her people. According to Persian law, she was not allowed access to King Ahasuerus unannounced. But because of the emergency, she prayed, fasted, and entered the chamber of the king. As she entered the presence of the greatest ruler of that time, the king graciously stretched out his scepter as a sign of approval. Eventually the Jews were spared and prospered through the intercessions of Queen Esther. If a Persian monarch rejoices to see his queen, *how much more* will your heavenly King rejoice to welcome you into His chambers!

We have access to a throne of grace! A King of love!

We live in a world in which everyone wants to be connected. Social media has tapped into a reality that has always existed. We want accessibility to friends. Jesus teaches through the parable of the persistent friend that God is both accessible and approachable.

When we link our lives to Him through prayer, He has promised to change our hearts. More and more our lives will start reflecting the kingdom of heaven. In our next chapter we will explore together what this looks like in practical life.

# Chapter 6

# A CHANGE OF HEART

The Parable of the Good Samaritan

Based on Luke 10:25-37

Corrie ten Boom lived with her family in Haarlem, the Netherlands, during World War II. As devoted Christians, the Ten Boom family recognized it was their duty and privilege to take care of Jews and others who had come under great threat. They opened their home and took in as many as they could. A secret room was prepared for the Jews and resistance workers, to hide when raids would take place.

On February 28, 1944, a Dutch informant told the Nazis about the Ten Booms' work, and that same day the entire Ten Boom family was arrested. They were sent to Scheveningen Prison, but the group of six people hidden by the Ten Booms remained undiscovered.

Later Corrie and her sister Betsie were sent to the Ravensbrück concentration camp, a women's labor camp in Germany. Betsie died at Ravensbrück, but Corrie returned to the Netherlands after the war. She set up a rehabilitation center in Bloemendaal that housed concentration-camp survivors and sheltered jobless Dutch people who had collaborated with the Germans during the occupation. The fact that Corrie reached out to those who were considered the enemy was controversial, but she earned the respect of many by her life of selfless service to everyone in need. Her life was marked by love for her neighbor. And she understood her neighbor to be anyone in need of the caring, loving, forgiving, and restoring power of God.

## WHO IS MY NEIGHBOR?

A parable that inspired Corrie to meet the needs of not only the deserving but undeserving was the parable of the good Samaritan. This story had a transformational effect on the way Corrie viewed people around her. It has done the same for thousands of people around the world. This amazing story invites us into a paradigm shift when it comes to the way we think about, and treat, those who are different from us.

"And behold, a certain lawyer stood up and tested [Jesus], saying, 'Teacher, what shall I do to inherit eternal life?'

"He said to him, 'What is written in the law? What is your reading of it?'

"So he answered and said, ' "You shall love the Lord your God with all your heart, with all your soul, with all your strength, and with all your mind," and "your neighbor as yourself." '

"And He said to him, 'You have answered rightly; do this and you will live.'

"But he, wanting to justify himself, said to Jesus, 'And who is my neighbor?'

"Then Jesus answered and said: 'A certain man went down from Jerusalem to Jericho, and fell among thieves, who stripped him of his clothing, wounded him, and departed, leaving him half dead. Now by chance a certain priest came down that road. And when he saw him, he passed by on the other side. Likewise a Levite, when he arrived at the place, came and looked, and passed by on the other side. But a certain Samaritan, as he journeyed, came where he was. And when he saw him, he had compassion. So he went to him and bandaged his wounds, pouring on oil and wine; and he set him on his own animal, brought him to an inn, and took care of him. On the next day, when he departed, he took out two denarii, gave them to the innkeeper, and said to him, "Take care of him; and whatever more you spend, when I come again, I will repay you." So which of these three do you think was neighbor to him who fell among the thieves?'

*"And he said, 'He who showed mercy on him.'*

*"Then Jesus said to him, 'Go and do likewise' "* (Luke 10:25-37).

The parable of the good Samaritan is triggered by a conversation between a certain lawyer and Jesus. The lawyer asked Jesus: *"Teacher, what shall I do to inherit eternal life?"* Jesus replied with a question: *"What is written in the law? What is your reading of it?"* The lawyer then quoted from the Shema, which we find in Deuteronomy 6. The command to love the Lord your God with all your heart, soul, and strength was at the very center of Jewish thought and worship. The lawyer connected this teaching with another teaching we find in Leviticus 19:18, which says: *"You shall love your neighbor as yourself."* Jesus strongly affirmed that the command to love God and love our neighbor is the way to the abundant life God has called us to. It is the path to eternal life. Not because we earn our way to heaven, but because God's transforming power fills us with a love that reaches out to our Creator and those He created.

In another place Jesus made it clear that His entire law, the Ten Commandments, are summed up in these two commands (Matthew 22:37-40). This makes sense, as the first four commandments deal primarily with our relationship to God, expressing and revealing our love to Him. The last six commandments lay the foundation for our relationships with people around us, revealing our love for our neighbor. The Ten Commandments can be distilled to two commandments: love God and love your neighbor. We have already discovered that our covenant with God involves these principles of love being written in our hearts.

In the days of Jesus the religious leaders focused primarily on their commitment to God, while downplaying the commandments dealing with their interactions with others. There was an ongoing discussion among the religious elite as to who constituted their neighbor. Leviticus 19 was interpreted in different ways and often understood to mean their own people, especially those they perceived to be blessed by God with health and wealth.

The lawyer, wanting to justify himself, asked Jesus: *"Who is my neighbor?"* Jesus then told the parable of the good Samaritan. Before we get to the part about the Samaritan, it is fascinating to note that the man who got beaten and was lying on the road half dead was not identified. Jesus said only: *"A certain man went down from Jerusalem to Jericho, and fell among thieves . . ."* We don't know if he was a Jew or a Gentile. We don't know if he was rich or poor. We don't learn anything about his social status in life. The only thing we do learn about him is that he needed help.

The fact that the wounded man was deliberately not identified by Jesus is brilliant!

Jesus was pointing to the fact that *"our neighbor"* is the very person who needs our help and love, despite who they are or where they come from.

Jesus continued the parable by turning the tables, as the ones who were expected to help (priest and Levite) didn't extend a loving hand, while the very one who was least expected to help (the Samaritan) reached out to the man in need. The lawyer who asked Jesus the question was obviously a religious person who had a knowledge of the Torah (first five books of the Bible). He possibly could have had priestly duties as well, and in that case he would have recognized himself in the story. The word *"neighbor"* suddenly took on a whole new meaning for him.

The Scripture says that he came to test Jesus, but through the parable he was being invited to trust Jesus. When we start trusting Jesus, we will be led to see our neighbor as the very ones Jesus sought to serve and love. We can't truly love God, whom we have not seen, without loving our neighbor, whom we can see.

Just as it was intentional that the wounded man was not identified in the parable, so it was intentional that the Samaritan was clearly identified. Again Jesus turned the tables, emphasizing the least-expected outcome of the story. Jesus made the most hated person of the day the hero of the story!

We are not told the reason the priest and Levite passed by the man who was clearly in desperate need. It might have to do with their perception of defilement. If they touched a dead person, they could not perform religious services and duties. It seems that their desire to keep a certain status triumphed over the clear duty that was before them. The guise of religiosity often kept the religious leaders in the days of Jesus from truly serving the needs of the people. A false narrative had emerged that in order to be committed to loving and serving God, one could neglect the needs of certain people.

## FROM STATUS TO SYMPATHY

Jesus chose a Samaritan as a hero for a purpose. The Jews hated the Samaritans. Their rivalry went back for centuries. Between 700 and 800 B.C. the Assyrian Empire had attacked Israel and deported the 10 northern tribes. They had the custom of repopulating conquered countries with conquered people from other nations. The Israelites who were left in the land married Gentiles who were brought there. This resulted in a mixed race and a mixed religion. This syncretism of pagan worship with the practices of the Israelites can be seen in the history of the Samaritans. Since the Samaritans were not welcome to worship in the temple in Jerusalem, they built their own temple on Mount Gerizim. This was considered a sacred site, as they believed it was there, rather than Mount Moriah, where the Jewish temple had been built, that God had revealed Himself to Abraham and Isaac.

This historic background explains the conversation between Jesus and the Samaritan woman at the well (John 4:1-26). The woman challenged Jesus regarding the right place to worship. Jesus shifted the conversation to the spirit of worship:

*"But the hour is coming, and now is, when the true worshipers will worship the Father in spirit and truth; for the Father is seeking such to worship Him. God is Spirit, and those who worship Him must worship in spirit and truth"* (verses 23, 24).

Jesus knew that true worship by true worshippers would lead to true unity. He had come to break down the wall that separated Jew and Samaritan. For the first time Jesus revealed Himself as the promised Messiah (verses 25, 26).

Through the parable of the good Samaritan Jesus was redirecting us from status to compassion. The priest and Levite had status but no compassion. The good Samaritan had no status, at least not in the eyes of the Jews; but he had compassion. We see in stark contrast the difference between a profession of religion and a practice of it. Jesus was not looking at the outward appearances, but at the heart. The same is true with the Samaritan woman at the well. Though devoid of any status, she was receptive to Jesus' revelation of Himself as the Messiah. All the while Jesus struggled to break through to the Jewish leaders in high authority.

During Jesus' public ministry He was often ridiculed by the religious leaders. At one point when they really wanted to discredit Him, they called Him a Samaritan:

*"Then the Jews answered and said to Him, 'Do we not say rightly that You are a Samaritan and have a demon?' "* (John 8:48).

This of course was a false accusation, as Jesus neither was a Samaritan and certainly did not have a demon. But these words reveal the animosity of the Jewish leaders against Jesus and Samaritans. Paradoxically, in the parable of the good Samaritan we have a picture of the ministry of Jesus. The priest and Levite were not revealing this picture, but the good Samaritan was. What he did on a small scale Jesus did on a large scale. Jesus came to seek and save the lost (Luke 19:10). Jesus was always on the lookout for the marginalized and downtrodden in society. The life of Jesus nullified the question *"Who is my neighbor?"* Jesus came to serve, and this encompassed absolutely everyone.

The first thing we learn about the good Samaritan is that when he saw the wounded man, he had compassion. But it did not stop there. His compassion led him to serve. The parable details what he did for the wounded man. The good Samaritan provided help that cost him and inconvenienced him. He poured oil and wine on the wounds of the man. He used his own animal to transport the man to an inn. He paid the innkeeper and promised to pay any bills connected to the stay of the wounded man. This is not just a little inconvenient situation to help an individual. The Samaritan went out of his way to provide all the help needed. And through the entire ordeal there was no promise of any reimbursement from the wounded man. There was no reciprocal arrangement.

## SELFLESS SERVICE

This micro story portrays the selfless service of Jesus on a macro level. Jesus did not immediately see the results of His enormous sacrifice for the human race.

In the book of Romans the apostle Paul writes:

*"For when we were still without strength, in due time Christ died for the ungodly. For scarcely for a righteous man will one die; yet perhaps for a good man someone would even dare to die. But God demonstrates His own love toward us, in that while we were still sinners, Christ died for us"* (Romans 5:6-8).

Christ took the first step. A sacrifice was provided with the hope that we will come to acknowledge what He has done for us. Once we do recognize His unselfish love, this very love is to fill our hearts. We start looking at people through the lens of the gospel.

Jesus continually surprised people with the way He treated those who were considered the outcasts and marginalized. One of the most known and appreciated teaching moments in the ministry of Jesus was the Sermon on the Mount. In Matthew's Gospel account this extraordinary sermon, recorded in chapters 5-7, is immediately followed by two astonishing encounters between Jesus and an outsider. It's as though the teaching of Jesus is being illustrated in real life.

Jesus is pictured coming down from the mountain after the sermon, and a multitude of people are with Him. Suddenly the people are frightened by the sight of a leper. Leprosy was one of the most dreaded sicknesses, and the moment a person got this disease they lost all status in life. They were separated from family and loved ones and declared unclean. Leprosy was considered a curse from God. The leper saw in Jesus His last chance of any change in his misery.

He cried out: *"Lord, if You are willing, You can make me clean"* (Matthew 8:2).

Jesus proceeded to do the unthinkable. He stepped forward and put His hands on the leper. There are other miracles in the Gospels in which Jesus merely says a word and an individual is healed. We will get to one of these miracles in just a moment. So Jesus obviously did not need to touch the leper in order to heal him. But He wanted to!

*"Then Jesus put out His hand and touched him, saying, 'I am willing; be cleansed.' Immediately his leprosy was cleansed"* (verse 3).

Jesus touched the untouchable! He broke the rules regarding defilement. This should have defiled Jesus, but instead it healed the leper.

I live in the countryside, where my family has a garden. Each fall we dig up our potatoes and put them in bags to store throughout the winter. We are always careful not to put any rotten potatoes together with the good ones. It is a simple law of nature that the bad ones will affect the good ones. It has never happened that the good potatoes cure the rotten ones. It works only one way!

However, with Jesus we witness something new. The defilement of sin and sickness has no power over Him. To the contrary, His restorative power overrides and reverses all else.

Jesus was not fearful of contamination or defilement regarding His contact with people. Matthew records the miracle of the leper and immediately launches into a second miracle. This time we encounter a Roman centurion who has a sick servant needing healing. The Jews hated the Romans, who they were subjugated under. And yet once again Jesus healed someone considered an outsider. This time Jesus merely spoke a word, not because He did not want to touch the servant, but because this miracle highlights the faith of the centurion in the life-giving words of Jesus (verses 5-13).

Both miracles remind us that Jesus reached out to all humanity. Jesus continually broke down the walls of separation that had been erected.

## CHANNELS OF BLESSINGS

The parable of the good Samaritan is one of Jesus' most known and loved parables, but it is also one of the most revolutionary and relevant parables in our time. In a world of division and polarization, in which humans were continually creating the ins and the outs, Jesus revealed how different His kingdom is. We are invited to love our enemies; to show compassion to those we think deserve it the least. This kind of love does not naturally exist in us.

Through the Fall, this world is broken and fractured, and our default mode is to create barriers between ourselves and others. This parable invites us to change our minds. It starts with a change of heart! An acknowledgment that we are all sinners in need of a Savior. An awareness that in a fallen world we all need the healing grace of Jesus. We are caught in the crossfire of sin and suffering and are affected and wounded by the enemy's darts of divisions.

In the light of the gospel, we can start looking at people around us in a whole new way. Everyone needs the healing only Jesus can provide. We can become channels of blessings as we convey this good news. Jesus has gone before us and provided us with an example of what this looks like. He has promised to give us the strength we need to follow in His footsteps.

I pray you are enjoying our journey in the world of the parables so far. We still have some exciting and relevant stories ahead of us. For now, I want to invite you to a wedding you don't want to miss.

More on this in our next chapter!

# Chapter 7

# DON'T MISS THE WEDDING!

## The Parable of the Wedding Feast

### Based on Matthew 22:1-14

Weddings are events that most people don't want to miss. A few years ago my wife and I attended the wedding of two dear friends. It was a summer day, and the ceremony was planned to take place outside. The forecast looked great, but soon dark clouds rolled in. As the bride walked down the aisle, it started raining. Not just a light drizzle, but more like a torrential downpour. Everyone got absolutely soaked to the bone!

The wedding was being livestreamed, and people around the world were following the service. Some family and friends of ours had gathered to watch the service, and once they saw on the screen what was happening, they started to pray. Everyone prayed for the rain to stop. When it was my 3-year-old's turn to pray, he simply said:

*"Dear God, let them have a good time in the rain!"*

It's funny what can come out of the mouths of young children.

However, there is good theology in that prayer. Circumstances are sometimes far from ideal in life, but with God's help we can make the best out of these challenging moments. The wedding ceremony shifted to plan B and ended up in a barn nearby. Despite the rain, we would not have wanted to miss a minute of the beautiful moment as our friends exchanged their vows to one another. Our motivation to be there was because of them. This meant a lot more than the setting.

## A REJECTED INVITATION

In the parable that we will be exploring in this chapter, we read about an invitation to attend the wedding of a mighty King. The story narrates how, despite this incredibly generous invitation, many refused to attend the wedding. Not only was it challenging to get people to come, but the parable also elaborates on the carelessness of one of the attendees who had no interest in wearing the provided wedding garment for the guests. The parable is a wake-up call. We are all invited to be part of something incredibly beautiful, and we shouldn't want to miss any moment.

*"And Jesus answered and spoke to them again by parables and said: 'The kingdom of heaven is like a certain king who arranged a marriage for his son, and sent out his servants to call those who were invited to the wedding; and they were not willing to come. Again, he sent out other servants, saying, "Tell those who are invited, 'See, I have prepared my dinner; my oxen and fatted cattle are killed, and all things are ready. Come to the wedding.' " But they made light of it and went their ways, one to his own farm, another to his business. And the rest seized his servants, treated them spitefully, and killed them. But when the king heard about it, he was furious. And he sent out his armies, destroyed those murderers, and burned up their city. Then he said to his servants, "The wedding is ready, but those who were invited were not worthy. Therefore go into the highways, and as many as you find, invite to the wedding." So those servants went out into the highways and gathered together all whom they found, both bad and good. And the wedding hall was filled with guests.*

*"'But when the king came in to see the guests, he saw a man there who did not have on a wedding garment. So he said to him, "Friend, how did you come in here without a wedding garment?" And he was speechless. Then the king said to the servants, "Bind him hand and foot, take him away, and cast him into outer darkness; there will be weeping and gnashing of teeth."*

*"'For many are called, but few are chosen' "* (Matthew 22:1-14).

The parable of the wedding feast is made up of two parts. The first part is about the invitation that is given to come to the wedding of the King and the result of this invitation being rejected. The second part deals with the man who attended the wedding but refused to wear the wedding garment.

By portraying a people who refused an important wedding

invitation, Jesus is speaking about the privilege the historic nation of Israel had forfeited. They were called to have a front seat to see what God wanted to do for the world through them. Sadly, the Old Testament reports how too often God's chosen people rejected the invitation of mercy that was sent to them. In the parable the very messengers of the King were ridiculed, reflecting the reality of how the prophets, who had been sent to Israel, had been treated.

In the first century a wedding invitation was almost obligatory. On top of that, we are talking about not just a common wedding but a royal one. By not coming to the wedding, one was questioning the King's authority. This was regarded as treason. However, the parable speaks of a second invitation that was sent out as the story intensifies. A second chance was given by the King. Another gracious invitation was extended to an unthankful people. This time the message was given that everything had been made ready.

The Scriptures are a story of God doing everything possible to connect with His chosen people. All provision for humanity to be saved eternally has been made available, but how few appreciate what God (the King) and Jesus (the Son) have done. The reactions in the parable range from indifference to outright hostility. Some of those who give the gracious invitation are killed. History is marked by the blood of many martyrs who simply invited people to the greatest wedding – the wedding between Christ and His people.

There is a prophetic element to the parable, as Jesus talks about the destruction of the city belonging to those who refused the invitation and killed the King's servants. The city of Jerusalem was destroyed in A.D. 70, after Jesus had been killed and His followers persecuted.

Finally, a third invitation was given. Now the invitation was no longer going to a specific group of chosen people. As Jesus spoke this parable, he knew that soon the gospel would go into the world, reaching people belonging to many different nations.

As we look back in history, we see how the gospel invitation has been spread. Today the invitation is still being given around the world. We are all invited to the wedding between Jesus, the bridegroom, and His people, the bride. This is a wedding you don't want to miss!

## CORNERSTONE

The story of the wedding feast is part of a string of parables that are connected. Matthew records the parable of the wicked vinedressers (Matthew 21:33-45) right before the parable of the wedding feast. Both these parables were taught in the presence of the religious leaders. Jesus was revealing how He had been rejected as the promised Messiah. These encounters happened only days before the crucifixion of Jesus. The scribes and pharisees were set on trying to discredit and remove Him. Jesus was no longer holding back anymore, and the parables contained a final call to repent and turn around.

The parable of the wicked vinedressers recaptured the history of Israel. Jesus spoke of a vineyard owned by a landowner. The vineyard was leased to vinedressers, but when the landowner sent servants to receive the fruit, they were beaten, killed, and stoned. The landowner eventually sent his son, who was also killed. At this point we don't have to wonder what this is all pointing to. This is the central story of the Scriptures, and the final part of the parable was about to be fulfilled. Jesus, the Son, would soon give His life for His people. Jesus challenged the hearers to consider through this parable what they were about to do. He referred to Himself as the chief cornerstone that was rejected (Matthew 21:42). The chief cornerstone was the most essential part of the foundation for the temple. The whole building relied on this. The temple had no value if Jesus as the Messiah was rejected.

Later Peter wrote about Jesus as the cornerstone:

*"Coming to Him as a living stone, rejected indeed by men, but chosen by God and precious, you also, as living stones, are being built up a spiritual house, a holy priesthood, to offer up spiritual sacrifices*

*acceptable to God through Jesus Christ"* (1 Peter 2:5).

Jesus is our cornerstone, and our lives are to be founded on His teaching.

## A LOVE STORY

In the parable of the wedding feast, Jesus was tapping into a wedding story that involved Himself and His chosen people throughout time. Both in the Old Testament and the New Testament God's people are pictured as the bride. The Old Testament story of Hosea is a living parable picturing the pursuit of God toward His wayward bride. The everlasting gospel is a love story that culminates in a wedding with Jesus, the Son of the King, as the bridegroom.

The Bible ends with an invitation to the wedding feast:

*"Blessed are those who are called to the marriage supper of the Lamb!"* (Revelation 19:9).

This biblical picture communicates to us the depth of the relationship Jesus longs to have with us. Marriage brings two people together as they share the joys and challenges of life. Jesus wants to be our life companion, guiding us to the place He has prepared for us.

## THE WEDDING GARMENT

The second part of the parable of the wedding feast was about the man without the wedding garment. The ending of this parable might at first glance seem harsh, but we need to look at the bigger picture of what was taking place here. The act of not wearing a wedding garment was more than just neglect. It was a willful act of defiance. The wedding garment had been provided by the king, but the man refused to wear it. He chose to wear his own garments and still came. This takes on a deep spiritual meaning. The Pharisees and scribes believed they could live a just and righteous life by so many things of their own making, but they did not want to receive Jesus as the Messiah.

Ellen White writes:

"When the king came in to view the guests, the real character of all was revealed. For every guest at the feast there had been provided a wedding garment. This garment was a gift from the king. By wearing it the guests showed their respect for the giver of the feast" (*Christ's Object Lessons*, p. 309).

The man without the wedding garment had no respect for the King or His Son, and he knew what he was doing was completely unacceptable. Jesus says that when he was confronted, he was speechless. Why? He had no reasonable argument to give, as there was no logical excuse for his action. The parable reveals the work of judgment. Before the final judgment takes place, there is an investigation. The Scriptures reveal that before Jesus comes back to this earth the second time, there will be an investigative judgment, revealing who will inherit God's kingdom. Those who wear the wedding garment are those who have accepted and applied the gospel in their lives.

From the same chapter in *Christ's Object Lessons*:

*"This robe, woven in the loom of heaven, has in it not one thread of human devising. Christ in His humanity wrought out a perfect character, and this character He offers to impart to us. . . . We live His life. This is what it means to be clothed with the garment of His righteousness"* (pp. 311, 312).

This concept of Christ's garment spans the entire story of Scripture. In the beginning Adam and Eve were clothed in a garment of light, but after they sinned, they were found naked. They hid themselves and sewed together fig leaves as garments (Genesis 3:7). This is a symbolic picture of righteousness by works. It was an attempt to fix things themselves, instead of trusting in God's plan. But it was not approved, and God provided garments for them by taking the life of an animal (verse 21). This pointed to the great sacrifice that was needed to "clothe" humanity. The plan of redemption is to clothe us in Christ.

The prophet Isaiah wrote:

*"I will greatly rejoice in the Lord, my soul shall be joyful in my God; for He has clothed me with the garments of salvation, He has covered me with the robe of righteousness, as a bridegroom decks himself with*

*ornaments, and as a bride adorns herself with her jewels"* (Isaiah 61:10).

Wearing the wedding garment is receiving the righteousness of Christ. It is receiving His character that He seeks to live out in us. Jesus wants to deal with our past (justification) and future (sanctification). He promises to forgive our past sins, but also to give us a new beginning. In this new life we are invited to live by faith, believing the promises of what God wants to do in us.

## THE POTTER AND THE CLAY

One of my favorite pictures of God in the Bible is found in Jeremiah 18. The prophet Jeremiah is told to go down to the potter's house. As he watches the potter at work with the clay, God speaks to him.

*"O house of Israel, can I not do with you as this potter?" says the Lord. "Look, as the clay is in the potter's hand, so are you in My hand, O house of Israel!"* (Jeremiah 18:6).

God reveals Himself as a potter. He wants us to be like clay in His hands. We can't change ourselves, but figuratively speaking, we can place ourselves in His hands and let Him shape us. As long as we are willing to be molded and fashioned by our Potter, a work of spiritual growth (sanctification) can take place. There will be moments we wrestle ourselves out of His loving hands, but once we are aware of this, we can again surrender and allow God to continue to mold us. In this beautiful process we let the Holy Spirit work in us as we seek guidance and direction in God's Word. God, as potter, wants to shape us into His image so that we can reflect the character of Jesus in our lives.

Too often this picture is turned upside down, and instead of God shaping us in His image, we create God in our own image. When humans become the potter and God becomes the clay, we get a picture of God that is devised in the human mind. This is why there are so many different religions in our world. Different people have different opinions about God. But Jesus asks us not to base our picture and understanding of God on our own ideas. Instead, He invites us to look to Him.

Jesus said to His disciples:

*"He who has seen Me has seen the Father"* (John 14:9).

Do you want to know what God is like? Look to Jesus! Here is our answer! Being shaped into the image of God is simply becoming more and more like Jesus. This is what the wedding garment is all about: allowing the character of Jesus to be displayed in our lives.

## THE ROBE OF RIGHTEOUSNESS

But for this to happen, Jesus must be allowed access into our lives. When we get to the last book in the Bible, the book of Revelation, there is a final call to the last church in the end of time. Revelation 2 and 3 contain seven letters written to seven churches in the first century. The disciple John, exiled on the island of Patmos, wrote to these congregations to encourage and direct them. Bible students have recognized that these seven letters not only are applicable to John's time but also are prophetic in nature. They span church history, from the first century till our day today. The seventh letter is especially relevant for our time. Jesus is directly addressing the needs of the church.

The picture we get of the seventh church, called Laodicea, is not flattering, to say the least. Jesus is directly quoted by John as saying:

*"Because you say, 'I am rich, have become wealthy, and have need of nothing'—and do not know that you are wretched, miserable, poor, blind, and naked"* (Revelation 3:17).

Here we find a church that thinks everything is OK, but it's not. Something is missing. They are described as "naked." This brings us back to a theme we have discovered in Scripture. God wants to clothe His people with His garments of salvation and robes of righteousness (Isaiah 61:10). But there must be a willingness to receive this gift. The man in the parable was offered a wedding garment, but he resolutely chose not to wear it.

This last church is also offered a gift:

*"I counsel you to buy from Me gold refined in the fire, that you may be rich; and white garments, that you may be clothed, that the shame of your nakedness may not be revealed; and anoint your eyes with eye*

*salve, that you may see. As many as I love, I rebuke and chasten. There-fore, be zealous and repent"* (verses 18, 19).

Jesus has all we need, and in love He reaches out to us. There is no need to remain in a state of self-righteousness. Jesus asks us to repent; to turn around and receive His restoring power in our lives. An attitude of faith and humility makes us like the clay that God, as our potter, can shape.

## WILL YOU OPEN THE DOOR?

Jesus ends the letter to Laodicea with these heart-stirring words:

*"Behold, I stand at the door and knock. If anyone hears My voice and opens the door, I will come in to him and dine with him, and he with Me. To him who overcomes I will grant to sit with Me on My throne, as I also overcame and sat down with My Father on His throne. He who has an ear, let him hear what the Spirit says to the churches"* (verses 20-22).

Jesus invites us to open the door. Notice that Jesus knocks, but we must open.

This door can be opened only from the inside!

This is an incredible scene that we need to consider as we come to the end of this chapter. Laodicea is outwardly religious, but has not opened the door to let Jesus in. We can be moral, decent, and religious without opening the door. We can even attend church and be active in ministry without letting Jesus into our hearts.

It's interesting that we even find reasons so that we don't need to open the door. Bear with my imagination for a moment. It's as if many are trying to get acquainted with Jesus by looking at Him through the keyhole in the door. A little glance now and then assures us that He is still there on the other side. We can go through all the religious motions, but never open our hearts to Christ. Through the keyhole we can whisper prayers and sing songs once a week, while still leaving Him outside of our ev-eryday lives. Even money can be slipped under the door to quiet our conscience as life continues. The reality is that religion can become a great place to hide from God when there is no personal relationship.

What then does it truly mean to be a Christian, a follower of Jesus? Ultimately, it's not the outward forms that answer this question. It all comes down to whether we have truly allowed Jesus access into our lives. On which side of the door is He? Is He outside or inside? This is the crucial, decisive matter. When Jesus is on the inside, He has become your treasure, more valuable than anything else. He has your greatest affections. He has your heart!

I love the way this is described by Ellen White:

"It is true that there may be an outward correctness of deportment without the renewing power of Christ. The love of influence and the desire for the esteem of others may produce a well-ordered life. Self-respect may lead us to avoid the appearance of evil. A selfish heart may perform generous actions. By what means, then, shall we determine whose side we are on? Who has the heart? With whom are our thoughts? Of whom do we love to converse? Who has our warmest affections and our best energies? If we are Christ's, our thoughts are with Him, and our sweetest thoughts are of Him. All we have and are is consecrated to Him. We long to bear His image, breathe His spirit, do His will, and please Him in all things" (*Steps to Christ*, p. 58).

I long to bear His image, and I believe you do as well. We will often fall short, but in those moments we shouldn't despair, as His grace and strength is always available. In this journey we are never alone! We have been promised a glorious ending.

God's people will be clothed and ready for the greatest wedding:

"'*Let us be glad and rejoice and give Him glory, for the marriage of the Lamb has come, and His wife has made herself ready.' And to her it was granted to be arrayed in fine linen, clean and bright, for the fine linen is the righteous acts of the saints. Then he said to me, 'Write: "Blessed are those who are called to the marriage supper of the Lamb!"' And he said to me, 'These are the true sayings of God'*" (Revelation 19:7–9).

You are invited! The table is set. The feast is made ready. A wedding garment has been provided.

It's up to us to show up!

# Chapter 8

# FILLED WITH THE SPIRIT

The Parable of the 10 Virgins

Based on Matthew 25:1-13

Some years ago I was scheduled to speak at a youth conference in Kuala Lumpur, Malaysia. I arrived in the evening and was scheduled to preach the following morning. Hoping to get some needed rest, I went to bed but could not sleep. Because of jet lag, my internal clock did not match my new destination. Many hours went by as I twisted and turned hoping to just get a doze, but to no avail. As the early-morning hours arrived, I considered it was better for me just to try to stay awake so I would not miss my first speaking appointment. I guess you can already predict what happened next.

Suddenly I was in a deep sleep, only to be awakened by the phone ringing in my room. The voice on the other end was clear *"Pastor Daniel, please come immediately. You are scheduled to speak in 15 minutes."* I jumped out of bed and got dressed in record time. Thankfully, the convention center was next to the hotel I was staying in. I ran through the corridors, and when I got closer to the auditorium in which I was going to speak, the host and tech guys were already running toward me. They miked me up while I was still walking. Moments later I was up on stage and starting my sermon. I am not sure if any of the attendees knew that I had just woken up from a deep sleep. I do know that I was happy that I had made it just in time!

Have you ever been almost too late for a very important appointment? The "almost" part is what caused your heart rate to rise. It's what gave you a shot of adrenaline and made you run faster to make it just on time. In this chapter we will look at a parable Jesus taught about being awake, present, and prepared not to miss out on His second coming, the greatest appointment of all!

## PREPARED FOR DELAY

Jesus again uses the analogy of a wedding:

*"Then the kingdom of heaven shall be likened to ten virgins who took their lamps and went out to meet the bridegroom. Now five of them were wise, and five were foolish. Those who were foolish took their lamps and took no oil with them, but the wise took oil in their vessels with their lamps. But while the bridegroom was delayed, they all slumbered and slept. And at midnight a cry was heard: 'Behold, the bridegroom is coming; go out to meet him!' Then all those virgins arose and trimmed their lamps. And the foolish said to the wise, 'Give us some of your oil, for our lamps are going out.' But the wise answered, saying, 'No, lest there should not be enough for us and you; but go rather to those who sell, and buy for yourselves.' And while they went to buy, the bridegroom came, and those who were ready went in with him to the wedding; and the door was shut. Afterward the other virgins came also, saying, 'Lord, Lord, open to us!' But he answered and said, 'Assuredly, I say to you, I do not know you.' Watch therefore, for you know neither the day nor the hour in which the Son of Man is coming"* (Matthew 25:1-13).

The parable of the wise and foolish maidens reflects some of the wedding customs that were practiced in the Holy Land at the time of Jesus. The wedding unfolded over several days. An important part took place when the bridegroom arrived at the bride's house to lead her back to his family's house. Many things could lead to the delay of the bridegroom arriving at the bride's house, or the delay of the wedding party heading back from the bride's house to the groom's house. A delay in a marriage procession was not only possible but very likely. In the parable the waiting time was so lengthy that all 10 maidens had fallen asleep. When the cry was heard that the bridegroom was arriving, all 10 maidens woke up. But only five of them had enough oil to relight their lamps. These are the ones who had prepared themselves for the conceivable and plausible scenario that things would take longer than expected.

This parable is given right after another parable that describes two servants (Matthew 24:45-51). Jesus told the story about a faithful and wise servant who was always ready for the return of his master. The wise servant was contrasted with an unwise and evil servant who said in his heart, *"My master is delaying his coming"* (Matthew 24:48). This servant was described as living in an immoral way.

Right after this story, Jesus launched into the parable of the wise and foolish maidens. The wise maidens were characterized by being ready for the coming of the bridegroom. The master and bridegroom in both these parables is a picture of Jesus and His coming back to this world. Some are prepared, while others are not. The foolish maidens were waiting for the bridegroom, but they were not prepared for the delay that took place. Their oil ran out. The wise had made provision for the possibility of delay, while the foolish had been short-sighted, and no careful and proper judgment of the event had been made.

The two parables make it clear that it is unwise both to live on the presumption that Jesus will delay His coming and to live with the expectation that Jesus will come so very soon that there is no watchful preparation to endure till the end.

## A MESSAGE OF HOPE

Both these parables come right after Jesus has given His famous end-time sermon, found in Matthew 24. Jesus was asked by His disciples what the signs of His coming would be and the end of the age. He revealed the signs that would increase in frequency and intensity as we get nearer to the end. There will be wars, famines, pestilences, earthquakes, and lawlessness. But amid all the bad news there will be good news.

Jesus said:

*"And this gospel of the kingdom will be preached in all the world as a witness to all the nations, and then the end will come"* (Matthew 24:14).

The gospel of Jesus is the light of the world. The maidens in the parable needed to have their lamps trimmed and burning. As followers of Jesus, we are called to spread a message of hope in a world that is becoming increasingly dark. This ultimate hope does not lie in some political solution, smart strategy, or advanced technology. It is rather rooted in a promise—the promise that Jesus will one day make all things right.

The biblical narrative ends on a happy note. If it's been a while since you read the last two chapters of Revelation, please remind yourself of the amazing future God has in store for us. If you have never read these chapters before, check them out!

However dark things are getting right now, this is not how things will continue forever. We will always be flanked by good news. The good news of the past is that Jesus came 2,000 years ago and gained a victory over sin and death. His resurrection assures us that there is hope. The good news of the future is that Jesus has promised to come back to this world. At His coming there will be a resurrection of all those who have put their trust in Him (1 Thessalonians 4:13-18).

## ASLEEP AT THE MOST CRITICAL TIME

As Jesus tells the story of the 10 maidens, He is illustrating the experience of the Christian church that will exist just before His second coming.

Through the parable He distinguishes between two classes of people who are waiting for His return. Jesus describes similarities and one major difference between the wise and foolish maidens. What they have in common is that they are all awaiting the coming of the bridegroom. This is a picture of the church looking forward to seeing Jesus. But then all 10 maidens fall asleep.

It's not the first time God's people are found sleeping at the most critical time. Three of the closest disciples of Jesus fell asleep just as Jesus appeared in all His glory on the Mount of Transfiguration. Later the same disciples fell asleep just as Jesus asked them to pray with Him in the Garden of Gethsemane. Jonah fell asleep on the ship carrying him away from the task God called Him to in Nineveh. Figuratively, the church today at times is sleeping when it should be awake and aware of the soon coming of Jesus and the task it has been given.

The apostle Paul admonishes the church:

*"And do this, knowing the time, that now it is high time to awake out of sleep; for now our salvation is nearer than when we first believed. The night is far spent, the day is at hand. Therefore let us cast off the works of darkness, and let us put on the armor of light"* (Romans 13:11, 12).

## FILLED WITH THE SPIRIT

Take note that all 10 maidens are awaiting the bridegroom. All 10 fall asleep during the time of waiting. All 10 wake up once they hear the bridegroom coming. All 10 had put oil in their lamps. The only difference was that the five wise maidens had extra oil in their vessels so they could refill their lamps. Had the bridegroom come earlier, no one would have noticed the difference between these two classes. It is the delay that reveals the distinction between the wise and the foolish.

The key teaching to the church today is that we need extra oil as we await the coming of Jesus.

The lamps symbolize the Word of God. The psalmist says:

*"Your word is a lamp to my feet and a light to my path"* (Psalm 119:105).

The oil is a symbol of the Holy Spirit that flows through the Scriptures. Oil was used to anoint prophets, priests, and kings.

When Jesus started His earthly ministry, He quoted from the book of Isaiah and said:

*"The Spirit of the Lord is upon Me, because He has anointed Me to preach the gospel to the poor; He has sent Me to heal the brokenhearted,*

to proclaim liberty to the captives and recovery of sight to the blind, to set at liberty those who are oppressed; to proclaim the acceptable year of the Lord" (Luke 4:18, 19).

Jesus was anointed by the Holy Spirit to fulfill His task on this earth. In the same way, we need to be filled with the Holy Spirit to accomplish our purpose as a church awaiting the coming of Jesus. This is truly our greatest need!

The parable of the wise and foolish maidens ends with the words:

*"Watch therefore, for you know neither the day nor the hour in which the Son of Man is coming"* (Matthew 25:13).

## THE BRIDEGROOM IS COMING!

We are to always be ready, and while we are waiting, we are to let our lamps shine brightly in this dark world. We have a beautiful message for all the world to hear:

The bridegroom is coming!

The Bible is full of promises that Jesus will return to this earth. It will be different from His first coming. He will not come as a babe in Bethlehem, but as King of kings and Lord of lords.

His coming is described as a glorious event that everyone will behold:

*"When the Son of Man comes in His glory, and all the holy angels with Him, then He will sit on the throne of His glory"* (verse 31).

In the book of Revelation we are told:

*"Behold, He is coming with clouds, and every eye will see Him, even they who pierced Him"* (Revelation 1:7).

This climactic event is not a secret that only a chosen few will see and hear. Everyone living on this planet at the time of His coming will see His splendid appearing.

## GOD'S ETERNAL KINGDOM

The phrase *"Son of Man,"* which Jesus uses in this parable but also in many other instances, is by far the most frequent way Jesus described Himself in the Gospels. The phrase appears in the prophetic Old Testament book of Daniel. In Daniel 7 we have a prophecy describing the coming of the ultimate King in the end of time. The prophet sees four beasts, representing four earthly kingdoms. These earthly powers are portrayed as conquering and subduing people. But then the scene suddenly changes, and the prophet Daniel sees the throne room of heaven. He beholds a judgment in favor of those who have been oppressed.

The Son of Man appears and is given a kingdom:

*"I was watching in the night visions, and behold, One like the Son of Man, coming with the clouds of heaven! He came to the Ancient of Days, and they brought Him near before Him. Then to Him was given dominion and glory and a kingdom, that all peoples, nations, and languages should serve Him. His dominion is an everlasting dominion, which shall not pass away, and His kingdom the one which shall not be destroyed"* (Daniel 7:13, 14).

The contrast between these earthly kingdoms and God's eternal kingdom, ruled by Jesus, could not be greater. The *"Son of Man"* did not come to oppress, but to uplift the weary. He came, not to be served, but to serve. He first wore a crown of thorns, revealing what He was willing to go through for us. He has won our allegiance and is the only one who deserves our worship. The *"Son of Man"* has united Himself with humanity. He left His glory to become one of us and to conquer sin and death on our behalf. When we put our faith in Him, we are linked with His eternal kingdom.

The *"Son of Man"* is the bridegroom who will soon pick up His bride, the church.

Jesus knew there would be enough in this world to trouble us, but He left us with an amazing promise. The promise of His return keeps us looking upward, knowing that in the end all things will be made right.

The disciple John recorded some of the most famous words of Jesus concerning this promise:

*"Let not your heart be troubled; you believe in God, believe also in Me. In My Father's house are many mansions; if it were not so, I would*

*have told you. I go to prepare a place for you. And if I go and prepare a place for you, I will come again and receive you to Myself; that where I am, there you may be also"* (John 14:1-3).

This is the language of an ancient Jewish wedding. The bridegroom would go and prepare a place for his bride. Once the place was ready, he would return to pick up his beloved bride. What a promise!

Just as Jesus has a special place prepared in heaven for you, so He also has a special task prepared for you on this earth. He has given each of us talents, skills, and opportunities, to be put to use in spreading the good news of the gospel.

In our next chapter we will explore the parable of the talents, revealing how much each of us matter in this final proclamation.

# Chapter 9

# YOU MATTER!

The Parable of the Talents

Based on Matthew 25:14-30

Nick Vujicic was born in 1982 in Melbourne, Australia. He had a rare disorder called tetra-amelia syndrome, characterized by the absence of all four of his limbs. Nick was born without arms and legs. He had two small feet, one of which had two toes. Nick became one of the first physically disabled students integrated into a mainstream school. However, his lack of limbs made him a target for bullying, and he fell into a severe depression. At age 10 he contemplated suicide and even tried to drown himself in his bathtub, but his love for his parents prevented him from following through. However, a key turning point in his faith came when his mother showed him a newspaper article about a man dealing with a severe disability. Nick understood he wasn't unique in his struggles and began to accept his lack of limbs. He realized his accomplishments could inspire others, and became grateful for his life. He gradually figured out how to live a full life without limbs, adapting many of the daily skills limbed people accomplish without thinking.

When Nick was 17, he started to give talks at his prayer group, and later founded his nonprofit organization, Life Without Limbs. This ministry is dedicated to reach out to the brokenhearted and to share the good news of Jesus Christ around the world. Nick, as a preacher and motivational speaker, has inspired millions of people. He famously said:

*"If God can use a man without arms and legs to be His hands and feet, then He will certainly use any willing heart!"*

God desires to use our talents, though they may seem few and insignificant, to bless and inspire people around us.

## DISTRIBUTION OF TALENTS

Jesus taught a parable that reminds us that our talents, resources, and opportunities are given us for a reason.

*"For the kingdom of heaven is like a man traveling to a far country, who called his own servants and delivered his goods to them. And to one he gave five talents, to another two, and to another one, to each according to his own ability; and immediately he went on a journey. Then he who had received the five talents went and traded with them, and made another five talents. And likewise he who had received two gained two more also. But he who had received one went and dug in the ground, and hid his lord's money.*

*"After a long time the lord of those servants came and settled accounts with them. So he who had received five talents came and brought five other talents, saying, 'Lord, you delivered to me five talents; look, I have gained five more talents besides them.' His lord said to him, 'Well done, good and faithful servant; you were faithful over a few things, I will make you ruler over many things. Enter into the joy of your lord.' He also who had received two talents came and said, 'Lord, you delivered to me two talents; look, I have gained two more talents besides them.' His lord said to him, 'Well done, good and faithful servant; you have been faithful over a few things, I will make you ruler over many things. Enter into the joy of your lord.'*

*"Then he who had received the one talent came and said, 'Lord, I knew you to be a hard man, reaping where you have not sown, and gathering where you have not scattered seed. And I was afraid, and went and hid your talent in the ground. Look, there you have what is yours.'*

*"But his lord answered and said to him, 'You wicked and lazy servant, you knew that I reap where I have not sown, and gather where I have not scattered seed. So you ought to have deposited my money with the bankers, and at my coming I would have received back my own with interest. Therefore take the talent from him, and give it to him who has ten talents.*

*"'For to everyone who has, more will be given, and he will have*

*abundance; but from him who does not have, even what he has will be taken away. And cast the unprofitable servant into the outer darkness. There will be weeping and gnashing of teeth' "* (Matthew 25:14–30).

The wider context of Jesus' teaching, prior to the parable of the talents, helps us better understand what the parable itself is about. Jesus, at this time, had come to the end of His earthly ministry. In Matthew 23 Jesus gave His final public appeal to the religious leaders. In the following chapter (Matthew 24) Jesus prophesied the destruction of the city of Jerusalem and pointed to the signs that would take place before His second coming. In the context of these end-time signs He taught a few parables, two of which are found in Matthew 25. In our previous chapter we looked at the parable of the wise and foolish maidens. It's about a wedding and the importance of being prepared for the arrival of the bridegroom. The bridegroom is Jesus Himself, who will return to be united with His people. The parable that follows is Jesus' teaching on the talents. A man is described as going on a journey to a faraway country, but eventually he returns. Jesus would ascend into heaven after His public earthly ministry had come to an end, but He had promised He would come back. Both parables revolve around a waiting time and how this time is filled. Right between the parables Jesus says: *"Watch therefore, for you know neither the day nor the hour in which the Son of Man is coming"* (Matthew 25:13).

## DEVELOPMENT OF TALENTS

The talents spoken of in the parable are monetary measurements. One talent was roughly equivalent to 6,000 denarii. One denarius was equivalent to one day's pay for an unskilled laborer. So to put this into perspective, one talent represented about 20 years of labor. One talent was an extraordinary amount, let alone five talents! The servants in the parable were entrusted with large amounts of resources to steward well. The servants with greater ability were entrusted with more money. In the spiritual application of the parable, we see how Jesus journeyed to a far country, a heavenly one, while giving us a task on this earth. He entrusted us all with talents. The "talents" He gave us are referring not only to our monetary means but also to all the abilities we have, and can improve, to bless people around us. Here the English word "talent" describes it well, referring to skills and natural abilities we have the opportunity to develop.

In parables a character in the story might represent God or Jesus, but the character is never a perfect representation. This is an important disclaimer, so that we don't put more into the characters than was intended. Though the man who gave the talents and traveled to a faraway land represents Jesus, there are significant differences. The man in the parable has given talents and requires an increase of these. So Jesus expects that we use the talents He has given us. But here is a truth that can free us in so many ways. Not only does the talent come from Jesus, but He also can increase the talent that comes from Him! We are not left on our own. Jesus wants to work in us and cultivate the very talents He has created us with.

The servant who got one talent in the parable was not required to produce five. He only had to increase that which he was entrusted with. God does not require more than for us to develop and improve the abilities He has given us in the first place.

Though God's love is equal to all, His giftedness varies from person to person. Without this understanding, we will live in either frustration or self-ease. The frustration rises when we live with the continual expectation that we should be doing something we were never gifted and equipped to do. We think we should produce five talents when we have received only one.

On the other hand, there is the danger of falling into self-ease. This is the comparison trap of doing the minimum, since others aren't doing as much as we are, while God has given us resources and talents to do far more. Both ditches are easy to fall into, but we can navigate our way forward when we keep our eyes on Jesus. He can give us the strength we need to work in the sphere He has placed us, with the opportunities He has provided us. In the end no one can boast, as everything comes from Him.

## OUR PICTURE OF GOD AND OUR ACTION POTENTIAL

The parable talks about the settling of accounts. The man in the parable returns to examine what his servants have done with the entrusted talents. Salvation comes by faith and not works, but our relationship with Jesus will result in a desire to serve and use our talents to reach others. Our works will be the fruit of our faith in Jesus.

*"Then he who had received the one talent came and said, 'Lord, I knew you to be a hard man, reaping where you have not sown, and gathering where you have not scattered seed. And I was afraid and went and hid your talent in the ground. Look, there you have what is yours"* (Matthew 25:24).

The servant with the one talent is afraid of the harshness of his master, and his fear of failing his master crippled his effectiveness. When we fear that we are not good enough for God to use us, we are doubting the power of God. We are saying that He can't do in us that which He has promised in His word He can do. Our picture of God is directly connected to our action potential. Remember that we serve, not a harsh master, but rather a loving Savior who wants us to flourish in life and be a blessing to others.

It often happens that when we feel we don't have much to give, we retreat and bury whatever we do have. We think that our contribution does not make a difference, while the significant truth of the parable is stating clearly: Yes, it does matter!

You, with the one talent, matter!

## SPIRITUAL GIFTS

When the apostle Paul wrote to the different churches he had raised up, he would remind them that all the members of the church were given spiritual gifts. These spiritual gifts were God-given abilities to help unite the believers and spread the gospel. The gifts were wide-ranging, from teaching and preaching to leadership and various forms of service.

I have witnessed again and again how God uses different individuals to build up the church spiritually. Some people have the special gift of hospitality and can create an atmosphere around them in which people thrive and long to be. Others are especially driven to intercessory prayer, and God uses them to soften hearts. Certain people have an anointing on their lives when it comes to proclaiming the gospel through their teaching and preaching. And then there are people who are born leaders and know how to bring the best out of others. There is a place for everyone, and God's plan is for all these spiritual gifts to create a synergy that can transform lives.

In 1 Corinthians 12 Paul likens the spiritual gifts activated in the church to a body with various members. All parts of the body are important for the body to function as it should.

Listen to what he says:

*"But now indeed there are many members, yet one body. And the eye cannot say to the hand, 'I have no need of you'; nor again the head to the feet, 'I have no need of you.' No, much rather, those members of the body which seem to be weaker are necessary"* (1 Corinthians 12:20-22).

The bottom line is: You matter! You really do!

Paul goes so far as to say that the health of the church is dependent on all its members discovering and activating their spiritual gifts. Just as the body is affected when one part suffers, so the church is weakened when talents are not utilized.

*"And if one member suffers, all the members suffer with it; or if one member is honored, all the members rejoice with it. Now you are the body of Christ, and members individually"* (verses 26, 27).

A church becomes defective when talents are buried. No wonder many churches around the world today are figuratively halting and limping along. They are barely surviving and certainly not thriving. The secret to turn this around is found in the parable of the talents.

## TRUE FULFILLMENT

But what makes someone want to use their talent rather than hide it?

We often pursue those things in life that give us joy and fulfillment. So the question we should ask ourselves is how we can find true happiness and purpose in exercising our talents for God. Once we have tasted the blessings that come from Christian service, we will be drawn back to it again and again. It will naturally become part of our DNA. It's who we are.

One of the things I love most in life is to be able to communicate and share the truths of the Bible. I have discovered that God aligned my passion and the spiritual gift He gave me. I find my purpose in life by being able to share the gospel and explain the Scriptures. This is not merely a job I do to make a living. Neither is it only a hobby I fill my free time with. It is literally the driving force of my life.

You might think that I was privileged to be born with communication skills, and therefore this was an easy deal. The truth, however, is that when I was growing up, I was terrified to speak in front of people. I remember being so nervous in high school whenever I had to speak up front. I would try to find all the reasons I could to prevent those moments from happening.

In my early 20s I knew I wanted to do something for God, and decided to attend a Bible college. Sure enough, one day I was assigned to speak for a morning chapel. I prayed and asked God to take away my fears of public speaking so that I could make it through this ordeal. Well, sometimes God answers our prayers way beyond what we can imagine or think. Not only did He give me confidence during that morning talk, but He placed within me a desire to preach. This passion developed into a preaching ministry that has brought me around the world.

Knowing my fears and uncertainties, I acknowledge that God did something supernatural in me. Therefore, all credit goes to Him. I received a spiritual gift, and I owe it to my God to use it for His glory. It continues to amaze me how pursuing God is also designed to give us maximal joy. God's ways are marvelous!

## UNHINDERED

What at times might keep us back from using our talents for God are circumstances we perceive as hindering us. However, sometimes the very circumstances that seem to hinder us can become catalysts to spread the gospel even further.

A prime example of this is once again the apostle Paul. As we get to the end of one of my favorite books in the Bible, the book of Acts, we read about the imprisonment of Paul in Rome. After all the miracles and divine leadings in the life of this apostle, he is now prevented from going to places he longs to proclaim the gospel. It almost appears that the whole story is going to end on a sad note. But Paul never allowed the conditions of life to prevent him from letting God's spiritual gifts flow through him.

Several of the letters we have in our New Testament today were written by Paul while in prison. So while he can't move around, his pen is still moving! Just think about the blessing his prison epistles have brought to millions of people throughout church history.

Paul used every opportunity he had to spread the good news of the gospel. When he first came to Rome, he was allowed to stay in his own rented house, though he was under continual supervision.

*"Now when we came to Rome, the centurion delivered the prisoners to the captain of the guard; but Paul was permitted to dwell by himself with the soldier who guarded him"* (Acts 28:16).

The Roman-Jewish historian Josephus, who lived in the first century, refers to prisoners most likely being bound to a soldier for a four-hour shift. As a preacher, I have a lively imagination, and so this gets me thinking as to how the soldier is experiencing this. I don't think Paul was silent about his faith during this time. He was continually inviting people over to his house to share the gospel:

*"So when they had appointed him a day, many came to him at his lodging, to whom he explained and solemnly testified of the kingdom of God, persuading them concerning Jesus from both the Law of Moses and the Prophets, from morning till evening"* (verse 23).

The soldier can't go anywhere while Paul is preaching his heart out!

Perhaps he really loved what he heard. Who knows whether after his four-hour shift he told his soldier colleague that he could take another shift. Perhaps when we get to heaven we will one day meet the Roman soldier who was chained to Paul. I know this is speculation, but the point is that Paul never let an opportunity to make a difference in someone's life pass. This was done even when all odds were turned against him. He was an unstoppable force for the kingdom of God.

The last verses in the book of Acts are fascinating. Paul is imprisoned, but God's Word is not!

*"Then Paul dwelt two whole years in his own rented house, and received all who came to him, preaching the kingdom of God and teaching the things which concern the Lord Jesus Christ with all confidence, no one forbidding him"* (verses 30, 31).

The book of Acts was originally written in Greek, and the last word recorded here is the word *akolutos*, which means "unhindered." What a way to end this story! Humanly speaking, things look dark, but from God's perspective we see opportunity.

Perhaps the very thing that you think is a hindrance for you to practice your spiritual gift can become the very thing that opens a door for you to spread the gospel. God is not dependent on your status in life. God can use your unique starting point as a means to bless others. Remember that in Christ you are unhindered!

## ENTER INTO THE JOY OF YOUR LORD

Once the master of the faithful servants in the parable returned, he welcomed his servants into the joy of the Lord.

*"Well done, good and faithful servant; you were faithful over a few*

*things, I will make you ruler over many things. Enter into the joy of your lord"* (Matthew 25:21).

The beauty here is that there is a great joy that awaits us when we devote our life to following our Lord and Savior. But this joy is not something that is designated only to the future. It can already start in the here and now. By allowing God to develop our spiritual gifts, we are increasing the talents He has entrusted us with. We can discover that increasing our talents and using them for God is the pathway to deep joy and purpose. It will involve a commitment, but it will be totally worth it!

I can't remind you enough that you matter. Your contribution is valued beyond what you can imagine. God has a plan for your life!

So let's go! There is a world to reach, and it starts with our neighborhood. Those we interact with and are within our sphere of influence. Let's pray that God fills us with His Holy Spirit and reveals to us how we can live to proclaim the gospel.

Life is short, and what we do today will matter throughout eternity.

In our next parable we will further explore this notion, as we are invited to live our lives in the light of what is to come.

# Chapter 10

# LIVING FOR ETERNITY

## The Parable of the Rich Man and Lazarus

### Based on Luke 16:19-31

Amy Carmichael was born in the small village of Millisle, Ireland, in 1867. She was the oldest of seven siblings and came from a well-off family. As a small girl Amy had once visited Belfast with her mother. During their time in the city they had stopped at a tearoom. As they ate, Amy noticed a grimy little beggar girl with her nose pressed up against the tearoom window. The poor little girl with no food was looking in at the rich little girl who had a plateful. The gaze in the girl's eyes affected Amy deeply. When Amy got back home, she sat down in front of the fireplace and wrote down a promise to the beggar girl:

*"When I grow up and money have,*
*I know what I will do,*
*I'll build a great big and lovely place*
*For little girls like you."*

As a young woman Amy Carmichael had a burden to help the poor women in the slums of Belfast. The women were nicknamed "shawlies" because they could not afford hats and would pull their shawls over their heads when they were out in the cold. Shawlies were not very welcome in church, so Amy fundraised and built a new meeting place for them called the Tin Tabernacle.

Later Amy moved to India, where she spent many years rescuing Hindu children from temple prostitution. Fulfilling her childhood dream, she provided a place of refuge for poor children. Under her leadership a hospital was built in Dohnavur, India, in 1913, providing care for many people that could not afford medical help. Amy lived her life for others who were less fortunate, and in doing so fulfilled the calling God had placed on her.

She famously said:

*"One can give without loving, but one cannot love without giving."*

## ETERNAL CONSEQUENCES

The parable we will look at in this chapter is about a rich man doing the very opposite of this selfless missionary. It's about a man who hoarded riches to himself and turned a blind eye to the obvious needs around him. We will discover how our lives today have eternal consequences for ourselves and others.

*"There was a certain rich man who was clothed in purple and fine linen and fared sumptuously every day. But there was a certain beggar named Lazarus, full of sores, who was laid at his gate, desiring to be fed with the crumbs which fell from the rich man's table. Moreover the dogs came and licked his sores.*

*"So it was that the beggar died, and was carried by the angels to Abraham's bosom. The rich man also died and was buried. And being in torments in Hades, he lifted up his eyes and saw Abraham afar off, and Lazarus in his bosom. Then he cried and said, 'Father Abraham, have mercy on me, and send Lazarus that he may dip the tip of his finger in water and cool my tongue; for I am tormented in this flame.' But Abraham said, 'Son, remember that in your lifetime you received your good things, and likewise Lazarus evil things; but now he is comforted and you are tormented. And besides all this, between us and you there is a great gulf fixed, so that those who want to pass from here to you cannot, nor can those from there pass to us.'*

*"Then he said, 'I beg you therefore, father, that you would send him to my father's house, for I have five brothers, that he may testify to them, lest they also come to this place of torment.' Abraham said to him, 'They have Moses and the prophets; let them hear them.' And he said,*

*'No, father Abraham; but if one goes to them from the dead, they will repent.' But he said to him, 'If they do not hear Moses and the prophets, neither will they be persuaded though one rise from the dead' "* (Luke 16:19-31).

The parable begins with Jesus painting a stark contrast between the unnamed rich man and Lazarus the beggar. Not only was the rich man rich, but he seemingly wanted everyone to know how wealthy and prosperous he was. He lived in extravagant luxury and showed off his wealth through his clothing and daily feasts. There is a clear focus on his outward appearance.

In the minds of many Jews in the first century, possessing wealth and health was directly connected to the fact that one was blessed by God. The rich Jewish man would have been highly esteemed in society. The beggar Lazarus, on the other hand, would have been looked down on. Many Jews would have argued that there must be a reason for all his suffering and unfortune in life. They believed that he must have sinned, resulting in God's curse and judgment being exposed in his misery.

This way of thinking is revealed in John 9, when the disciples asked Jesus about a blind man:

*"Rabbi, who sinned, this man or his parents, that he was born blind?"* (verse 2).

Lazarus was at the very bottom of society, fully dependent on the mercy of others. In addition, he would have felt the condemnation that rested on individuals like him.

However, in the parable there is a complete reversal of roles. This reversal sets in at death. Lazarus the beggar is carried to Abraham's bosom, while the rich man ends up in the torment of Hades. The unexpected takes place, and Jesus in the parable reveals that an outward appearance of riches cannot be equated with God's blessing. Neither can the suffering of a person be associated with God's curse. The beggar Lazarus, though he had a life of hardships, trusted God and was on his way to heaven. The rich man, with a life of ease, trusted in his own wealth and status, and in doing so was sealing his eternal destiny.

It is interesting to note that in the parable Lazarus is named, but the rich man is not. The name Lazarus is immortalized, but we don't know the name of the prosperous, influential rich man. He certainly made a name in this life, but in light of eternity he will be forgotten. In this parable Jesus reveals that it is in this life we decide our eternal destiny. Outward appearance is not what matters. What matters is where our heart is and in whom we trust.

## WHAT HAPPENS AFTER DEATH?

It is obvious that Jesus is using metaphors in the parable of the rich man and Lazarus. The point of the parable is not to give a detailed description of the afterlife, but rather to show how the decisions we make today impact our eternal destinies. Several observations make it clear that Jesus was not giving us a literal description of what happens when a person dies. Abraham's bosom would not be big enough for all the redeemed. A drop of water wouldn't help a person in flames. There are simply no Scripture passages that support the idea of a lost person communicating with a saved person after death.

The Bible pictures humans as mortal beings and death as an unconscious sleep until the resurrection takes place at the end of time.

Unfortunately, there is a lot of confusion within Christianity on the topic of death and the afterlife. This is because of the Greek Hellenistic idea of an immortal soul, which has made its way into Christian thinking. The Greeks, along with many other ancient civilizations, believed in an immediate afterlife at death. This is often termed *anthropological dualism*. It's the view that the human is made up of two components: a material, physical body and an immaterial soul or spirit. The soul is locked in the body, but at death it is as if the prison house is opened and the soul is released to live on forever and ever.

Hebrew thinking is very different than Greek thinking, and the Scriptures are passed down to us through Hebrews. Both the Old and New Testament do not support the idea of an immortal soul.

According to the Bible, there is only one who is immortal. Speaking of Christ, we read:

*"He who is the blessed and only Potentate, the King of kings and Lord of lords, who alone has immortality, dwelling in unapproachable light, whom no man has seen or can see, to whom be honor and everlasting power. Amen"* (1 Timothy 6:15, 16).

This does not mean that there is no hope for eternal life. There is one who has immortality, but there are others who receive immortality as a gift. We have promises in the Bible that there will be a resurrection in the end of time when Jesus comes back. This is when we experience the gift of eternal life.

Logically, we can ask the question: Is the soul immortal, or is there a resurrection? It does not make sense for both to be true at the same time. You will not need a resurrection if people go straight to heaven when they die.

Here is one of my favorite resurrection promises:

*"But I do not want you to be ignorant, brethren, concerning those who have fallen asleep, lest you sorrow as others who have no hope. For if we believe that Jesus died and rose again, even so God will bring with Him those who sleep in Jesus. For this we say to you by the word of the Lord, that we who are alive and remain until the coming of the Lord will by no means precede those who are asleep. For the Lord Himself will descend from heaven with a shout, with the voice of an archangel, and with the trumpet of God. And the dead in Christ will rise first. Then we who are alive and remain shall be caught up together with them in the clouds to meet the Lord in the air. And thus we shall always be with the Lord. Therefore comfort one another with these words"* (1 Thessalonians 4:13-18).

What a hope! And what a comfort! Death does not have the final word. Jesus has overcome the grave, and so will those who believe in Him.

We will one day dwell with Him. Not as a soul floating in heaven, but as a wholistic being. We exist within a body. This is the way we were created, and this is the way we will be recreated at the resurrection.

*"So when this corruptible has put on incorruption, and this mortal has put on immortality, then shall be brought to pass the saying that is written: 'Death is swallowed up in victory' "* (1 Corinthians 15:54).

The Christian's hope lies not in an inherent immortal soul, but rather in the victory of Christ, who rose from the grave and promised a resurrection. He imparts the gift of eternal life!

## ETERNAL TORMENT?

The doctrine of an immortal soul that continues to exist at death, without a body, is a Greek concept. This idea of an immortal soul is connected to the doctrine of an eternal hell. When you put something immortal into flames, it will burn forever. Though the Bible speaks about a final destruction of the lost, it does not teach eternal torment.

The disciple Peter writes:

*"And turning the cities of Sodom and Gomorrah into ashes, condemned them to destruction, making them an example to those who afterward would live ungodly"* (2 Peter 2:6).

Sodom and Gomorrah were destroyed by fire, but are not burning today. The false doctrine of an eternal hell puts God in a very bad light and has been the cause of many leaving Christianity. They cannot conceive of a loving God who would burn people in hell forever and ever. The good news is that the Scriptures do not support this view either. God is just, and His final judgment is fair.

The parable of the rich man and Lazarus was designed, not to teach details about the afterlife, but rather point to the decisions we make in this life. Jesus makes it very clear that the choices we make in this life cannot be reversed after death. There is no second probation. In the parable "a great gulf" is fixed between the rich man and Lazarus. The main point is that this life is the only time given to us in which to prepare for eternity.

## ABRAHAM, MOSES, AND THE PROPHETS

At the end of the parable Jesus describes a scene in which the rich man begs Abraham to send Lazarus to warn his five brothers, lest they also come to the same place of torment. Abraham responds: *"They have Moses and the prophets; let them hear them."* The rich man does not think that this will suffice and says to Abraham that when one from the dead goes to them, they will repent; to which Abraham answers: *"If they do not hear Moses and the prophets, neither will they be persuaded though one rise from the dead"* (Luke 16:27-31).

This is a fascinating dialog, and though this conversation did not literally happen, Jesus is giving us an insight into His own ministry and how it would be rejected by the religious leaders. The rich man in the parable is a picture of the nation of Israel. They were rich in the way that God had especially blessed them with oracles of truth to be shared with the surrounding nations. But just as the rich man in the parable had refused to share with the beggar, so Israel at large had not reached out to the nations around them with the incredible revelations of Scripture they had been entrusted with. Israel was surrounded by beggars— people longing for light.

The religious leaders believed they were better than others because they were descendants of Abraham.

John the Baptist warned them:

*"And do not think to say to yourselves, 'We have Abraham as our father.' For I say to you that God is able to raise up children to Abraham from these stones. And even now the ax is laid to the root of the trees. Therefore every tree which does not bear good fruit is cut down and thrown into the fire"* (Matthew 3:9, 10).

And Jesus Himself said to them:

*"If you were Abraham's children, you would do the works of Abraham. But now you seek to kill Me, a Man who has told you the truth*

*which I heard from God. Abraham did not do this"* (John 8:39, 40).

No wonder Jesus intentionally mentioned Abraham in the parable, and pictures the rich man separated from the very one he admired. Abraham was a rich man, but had a heart for the poor and needy. His life of faith was an example that the rich man in the parable, and Israel at large, failed to follow.

In the parable, Abraham pointed out twice that the brothers of the rich man had Moses and the prophets. Jesus on another occasion made a startling statement to the Jews when He said:

*"For if you believed Moses, you would believe Me; for he wrote about Me. But if you do not believe his writings, how will you believe My words?"* (John 5:46, 47).

The Jews failed to see Jesus as the promised Messiah and fulfillment of Scripture. The last words recorded in the parable are Abraham telling the rich man that if his brothers are not heeding Moses and the prophets, neither will they be persuaded if someone rises from the dead.

I don't think it is a coincidence that the crowning act of Christ's ministry was raising a man by the name of Lazarus from the dead (John 11). But this did not persuade those who were set on removing Jesus. After the crucifixion of Jesus on Friday, He rose from the grave on Sunday morning. But sadly, even this miracle of miracles did not bring repentance, confirming the very words of Jesus in the parable.

The name Lazarus comes from the Hebrew name "Eleazer," which means "God has helped." This is a reminder that all who seek help and refuge in God will find it in Christ. We encounter Christ in all His beauty in Moses and the prophets, the Word. Whatever hardships we go through in this life, we have the promise that one day all things will be made new. We have been promised an eternity with Jesus.

## "JUST IN CASE" THEOLOGY

I must admit that it is easy to at times lose this focus. Our attention goes to the here and now, and we forget what is to come. Or we compartmentalize God's promises of an eternal life from the "real" world we live in. Let me explain what I mean. I actually came up with a name for this. I call it the *"just in case"* theology. It's an unfortunate way of thinking that many have bought into. It works like this: We somewhat believe in God's promise of an eternal life, but "just in case" it is not true, we also want to get the best out of this present life. So what ends up happening is that we live for the here and now, revealed by our priorities and choices, but quiet our conscience by perhaps attending church now and then, or keeping some formal traditions that still link us to the Christian life. We compartmentalize what we perceive to be the "real" world from God's world, keeping one foot in each camp *"just in case."*

But the reality is that this mental compartmentalization is founded on a false premise. There are no "two worlds," but only one. God is real, and eternal life is real. The supernatural exists, though we don't always see it with our physical eyes. By faith we can still fully believe what the Bible reveals. Our experience with God in the here and now reminds us that He is present in our trials and seeks to guide us through life. His promises are real, and we can know that His strength is available. The Christian life is based on not only a future hope but a present experience with Jesus.

Sometimes our eyes need to be opened to this reality.

There is a fascinating account in the Old Testament about the prophet Elisha, who forewarns the king of Israel each time the Syrian army attacks. The prophet tells the king of Israel exactly where the enemy soldiers will show up, and each time Israel is prepared to defend itself. The king of Syria believes there must be a spy, but then learns about the predictions of Elisha. He reasons that the best thing he can do is get rid of the prophet. A great army is sent to Dothan, where Elisha is staying. The servant of Elisha first sees the horses, chariots, and soldiers. He cries out to the prophet "Alas, my master! What shall we do?"

What happens next is mind-blowing!

*"So he [Elisha] answered, 'Do not fear, for those who are with us are more than those who are with them.' And Elisha prayed, and said, 'Lord, I pray, open his eyes that he may see.' Then the Lord opened the eyes of the young man, and he saw. And behold, the mountain was full of horses and chariots of fire all around Elisha"* (2 Kings 6:16, 17).

God had sent an army as well! His protective angels had surrounded the prophet.

Just as the eyes of the servant were opened through prayer, so our eyes of faith need to be activated as we seek God. Through our study of the Scriptures our eyes are spiritually opened. We start seeing things we had not seen before. Some of the greatest realities are not seen with our physical eyes. But as we allow the great narrative of Scripture to unfold before us, we get a new perspective.

We start living in the light of eternity!

# Chapter 11

# THE ELEVENTH HOUR

The Parable of the Workers in the Vineyard

Based on Matthew 20:1-16

A friend told me about an experience she had had growing up that positively impacted her understanding of salvation and picture of God. Her father liked to give her special treats when she was helpful in the home. One day there was a lot to clean up, so he promised that they would go out for lunch and eat pizza together once the job was done. My friend told me how she didn't feel like helping that day, but was very interested in the pizza, and thought her dad would understand. Once the job was done, without her help, her dad invited her along to the pizzeria. She thought she had managed quite well to get her will. To her surprise, her dad ordered only one pizza. She thought that perhaps he was not hungry and that she would be enjoying the food alone. But once the pizza arrived, he placed it in front of himself and said that since she had not helped with the task that needed to get done that day, he would enjoy the pizza alone. Her first thoughts were: *How can he do this to me? This is not fair!* But suddenly she realized that she hadn't kept her side of the deal.

Her father smiled at her and pushed the pizza toward her and said that he would take the consequences of her actions by letting her enjoy his pizza. She shared how this experience made the gospel come alive. Jesus took our sins so we can be rewarded with grace, something we did not deserve. My friend had also gained a new perspective on being a helping hand in the home. We serve, not to get what we want, but out of gratefulness.

## JUST WAGES

In this chapter we will look at a parable that tells of God's reward of grace. The story also reveals our calling to serve in God's great vineyard. We all have a special place where we can make a difference to people around us. Jesus calls us to trust Him as we step out in faith, allowing the gospel to shine through us.

*"For the kingdom of heaven is like a landowner who went out early in the morning to hire laborers for his vineyard. Now when he had agreed with the laborers for a denarius a day, he sent them into his vineyard. And he went out about the third hour and saw others standing idle in the marketplace, and said to them, 'You also go into the vineyard, and whatever is right I will give you.' So they went. Again he went out about the sixth and the ninth hour, and did likewise. And about the eleventh hour he went out and found others standing idle, and said to them, 'Why have you been standing here idle all day?' They said to him, 'Because no one hired us.' He said to them, 'You also go into the vineyard, and whatever is right you will receive.'*

*"So when evening had come, the owner of the vineyard said to his steward, 'Call the laborers and give them their wages, beginning with the last to the first.' And when those came who were hired about the eleventh hour, they each received a denarius. But when the first came, they supposed that they would receive more; and they likewise received each a denarius. And when they had received it, they complained against the landowner, saying, 'These last men have worked only one hour, and you made them equal to us who have borne the burden and the heat of the day.' But he answered one of them and said, 'Friend, I am doing you no wrong. Did you not agree with me for a denarius? Take what is yours and go your way. I wish to give to this last man the same as to you. Is it not lawful for me to do what I wish with my own things? Or is your eye evil because I am good?' So the last will be first, and the first last. For many are called, but few chosen"* (Matthew 20:1-16).

It was not an uncommon scene to see laborers standing in the marketplace waiting to be employed for the day. Jesus pictures a scenario that the people could relate to. Perhaps some in the crowd listening to the parable of Jesus had themselves been workers in the position of waiting and hoping to get a job. Once a person was picked up by a landowner, an agreement would be made regarding wages. In the parable the first group working from the beginning agreed on a denarius a day. This was very reasonable, as it was considered a day's wage for unskilled workers in the first-century context of Judea.

Only a few hours into the day the landowner realized he needed more workers to complete the work that remained. Back at the marketplace the landowner found more laborers *"standing idle."* This expression does not mean that they were lazy, but merely that they had not yet received an invitation to work for anyone. The opportunity for work was simply lacking. Immediately after the invitation was given, those workers entered the vineyard. This scene repeated itself the sixth, ninth, and finally eleventh hours.

There was a big difference between the first workers and those coming in later during the day. It wasn't just that they had a shorter workday. The real difference was that they didn't have a work contract. They didn't know what they were going to earn, but they trusted the landowner, who said: *"I will give you whatever is right."*

Would you enter such a work contract today?

I guess it would depend on if it was "right" for you or your employer. We would most likely be left with some questions before entering such an agreement. But it would be different if you knew the employer to be a very fair, honest, and extremely generous person. Then the statement *"I will give you whatever is right"* would be inviting.

The parable takes on a deeper meaning when we identify God as the landowner. He invites us to work in His vineyard, which is the world. According to Jesus, there is a work to be done in spreading the gospel to all nations before the end comes (Matthew 24:14).

The first to be invited to spread a knowledge of God's character were the Israelites as a nation. The outcome and reward of their actions were clearly outlined in blessings and curses (Deuteronomy 28). They knew what they could expect. Some Israelites heeded the call, but sadly many did not. Later the call to "work in the vineyard" was extended to other people groups. They would receive "whatever is right." This invitation is given to all who receive Jesus as their Messiah, and the agreement is based on trust.

The parable speaks to us today. When we respond to the call to work in God's vineyard, He takes care of us. We all have a sphere of influence that can be used to spread the good news about Jesus.

So what are the right wages?

A few seconds into eternity we will all know that God gives what is right!

Eternity is our reward, and it is equally available for all. However, the joy of service can already start now. Our reward also involves the wonderful experiences we gain with Jesus when sharing His love with others.

## UNDESERVED

Toward the end of the day the landowner in the parable realized he needed more laborers to finish the work. He went back to the market one last time to invite those who are still waiting and willing to enter the vineyard. The eleventh-hour workers entered the fields only for the last hour of the day. The parable ends in a remarkable and unexpected way. The landowner could have first paid the laborers who had been there all day. They would have happily received the denarius they agreed on and left without knowing anything else. Instead, the landowner made them stand in the back of the line, only to see the eleventh-hour workers receive the same payment as was promised them.

How would you have responded if you had worked all day? Your first reaction would probably be to do some simple math. One hour equals one denarius, so 12 hours equals 12 denarii!

But when reality hits and you get one denarius, what is your next reaction? *This is not fair!* That was exactly the response of the laborers who got picked up the first hour.

The parable reveals a simple and extremely important principle of the gospel. We cannot earn our reward! It is simply a reward of grace, and it is equal for all who respond to the call of Jesus in their lives. In essence no one deserves anything, as salvation is a pure gift to be received by faith, not by works (Ephesians 2:8).

Remember the parable of the prodigal son. He leaves and squanders everything, only to return to his father, who organizes a feast. The older brother is very upset, as it does not seem to be fair.

We can either live our lives on a contract basis with God, expecting rewards for our work, or we can enter into a covenant with Him, trusting and knowing that He will always give what is right. In a relationship of trust, we will start recognizing the reward that is available to us all. We get to be a part of spreading the best news in the universe. And while we are doing so, Jesus has promised to be with us.

The discontentment sets in when we don't consider other workers on our team. If the goal is a completed work in the vineyard, it does not really matter who gets what. Our focus shifts to *"we finished the work,"* and the first workers can rejoice with the eleventh-hour workers.

If the goal is salvation, then let's celebrate every prodigal son! What a freeing way to live when we can simply trust our employer with *"whatever is right"*!

The parable stretches over a day of 12 hours. The eleventh-hour workers are, in a special way, called to help all the other workers finish the job. It is fascinating to think of this parable as stretching over the history of this world. Bible prophecy is fulfilling before our eyes, showing us that the second coming of Jesus is approaching.

We are figuratively living in the eleventh hour of this world's history!

I believe we can find ourselves in this parable. We are all called to use our talents and spiritual gifts to proclaim the gospel to the world. We are invited to join the work in the vineyard as eleventh-hour workers. Perhaps you find yourself still waiting in the marketplace. Waiting to be hired or looking for opportunities to serve. Take a step in faith and ask God where you can serve best in your local setting.

God has a special place for you in His vineyard!

## BUILDING GOD'S KINGDOM

For hundreds of years the Hebrews were slaves of the Egyptians. During this time God's chosen people were forced to produce bricks for Pharaoh. They worked long, hard days to make bricks that built up a kingdom that oppressed them. The more they worked, the mightier their enemy became.

But then God intervened. He sent Moses to set His people free. Through many divine miracles the Hebrews were led out of bondage and into liberty. While in the wilderness, on their way to the Promised Land, God wanted to manifest His presence among them and asked the people to build Him a sanctuary. The purpose of this special place was for God to dwell with His people (Exodus 25:8).

The work began, and the people gathered material for the building of the sanctuary. Two men named Bezalel and Aholiab were appointed as gifted artisans to oversee this work, while all the people were called to participate in the project. They once again became builders, but in a very different setting. In Egypt they were forced into labor to build an empire who hated everything they loved and stood for. Now they had experienced God's divine plan in setting them free. As a freed people, they were invited to once again build something. But this time they were not to build an earthly empire, built on oppression and injustice; rather, they were to build a representation of God's eternal kingdom, founded on truth, righteousness, and perfect justice. Their gratitude and appreciation toward their God, who had set them free, moved them to want to build Him a sanctuary.

The sanctuary itself pictured through types and symbols how God would ultimately liberate humanity from the slavery of sin.

Though there were many dark and unfortunate chapters in the story of ancient Israel, this was a happy moment. The story of Exodus tells us that the people were so enthusiastic in contributing to the sanctuary that it came to a point that Moses had to command the people to stop bringing materials for the building project. There was already too much. Sounds like a good problem! (Exodus 36:6, 7).

What are we building today? Is all our time and energy put into producing "bricks" for the kingdom of this world? Or are we, as a delivered people, building God's kingdom?

## LOOKING UNTO JESUS

The call to labor (and the reward of grace) revealed in the parable is really a revelation of how God's kingdom works. Those who responded to the call were to trust the landowner, as we are to trust God's dealings with us today.

The key is to look unto Jesus. Some of the workers in the parable became frustrated when they compared themselves with others. The moment our eyes are removed from Jesus and focused on others, we miss the amazing reward Christ has entrusted us with.

The Gospels contain the story about Peter, who is in a boat, while Jesus is seen walking on the Sea of Galilee. Jesus invites Peter to come to Him, and by faith he begins walking on the water. But the moment he takes his eyes off Jesus and looks at the other disciples, and the waves around him, he begins to sink. Jesus graciously pulls the wet disciple into the boat.

There are many things in life that can cause us to "sink," but they all have one thing in common. They take our eyes off Jesus.

One of the main reasons I am drawn to the parables is that they invite us to look to Jesus. Each parable is a window providing a new view into His life and character.

Before my wife, Silvia, and I were married, we were once hanging out with a group of friends when someone asked what our favorite Bible verse was. One by one we shared a text of Scripture that had impressed us in a special way. Silvia and I both immediately thought of the exact same Bible passage. It's found in the book of Hebrews:

*"Therefore we also, since we are surrounded by so great a cloud of witnesses, let us lay aside every weight, and the sin which so easily ensnares us, and let us run with endurance the race that is set before us, looking unto Jesus, the author and finisher of our faith, who for the joy that was set before Him endured the cross, despising the shame, and has sat down at the right hand of the throne of God"* (Hebrews 12:1, 2).

Looking unto Jesus! This is the ultimate key to a joy-filled purposeful life. It doesn't mean life will always be easy. However, we will always have someone to go to when storms arise. Waves will still crash around us, but our eyes will be fixed on the One who can keep us afloat. Keeping our eyes on Jesus will enable us to finish the work Jesus has called us to do in His vineyard.

## FINISHING THE RACE

At times this idea of *"finishing the work"* is also revealed as *"finishing a race,"* such as the text we just read in Hebrews 12.

When Paul wrote his last letter to Timothy, a fellow gospel worker, he looked back on his life of service and recorded:

*"For I am already being poured out as a drink offering, and the time of my departure is at hand. I have fought the good fight, I have finished the race, I have kept the faith. Finally, there is laid up for me the crown of righteousness, which the Lord, the righteous Judge, will give to me on that Day, and not to me only but also to all who have loved His appearing"* (2 Timothy 4:6-8).

Paul looked forward with confidence to His final reward. Why? Because he could look back on a life lived in service. He had trusted Jesus and kept his eyes on Him till the very end. He had completed the race that was set before him.

There is a great race that we are all part of. It's like a relay race. Paul passed the baton to the hands of Timothy. Timothy ran his race and passed on the baton to the next generation of gospel workers. Many centuries have passed, and the baton is now being given to us.

What are we going to do with it?

It is good to, at certain times in our lives, press the pause button for a moment. As we pause, we can ask ourselves some deep and important questions.

What do I want to do with the life God has given me? What do I want to accomplish with the years I will spend on this planet? Am I running the race that matters? Am I fighting the good fight that matters? Will I in 10, 20, 30, or 40 years from now be able to look back on my life with satisfaction?

And when you have a clear vision ahead of you, press the play button and run the race set before you, looking unto Jesus!

Your journey is an ongoing one.

However, our journey together, taking a closer look at Jesus' parables, is coming to a close.

But there is still one more parable that I want to share with you. It's a story that brings together all the incredible parables we have explored together in this book.

So stay tuned! I will be waiting for you in our last chapter!

# Chapter 12

# BUILDING ON THE ROCK

## The Parable of the Wise and Foolish Builder

## Based on Matthew 7:24-27

S ome people refer to it as the end of the world.

Its natives call it *"Aotearoa,"* meaning *"the land of the long white cloud."* More recently tourists describe it as *"middle earth."*

It's the only country I know of that has literally been forgotten on certain maps (don't ask me why).

For me, it's the place I was born. My first home. My first childhood memories.

New Zealand!

With its epic and contrasting scenery, it is both spectacular and charming. I like to describe it as the best of the world put together on an island in the middle of nowhere. You will find high snow-clad mountains, stunning fjords, volcanoes, rainforests, lakes, golden sand beaches, and endless rolling green pastures . . . with lots of sheep.

In my humble opinion the natural beauty is probably the closest you can get to heaven on this earth.

But New Zealand is known for something else. Something not as idyllic.

Earthquakes!

Situated on a fault line, known as the ring of fire, New Zealand is prone to quakes. Below the surface of this beautiful island there are active tectonic plates, causing the earth to shake.

I will never forget landing in Melbourne, Australia, on the February 22, 2011. Together with my wife, I was on my way to New Zealand for a speaking appointment. We were only going to transit in Melbourne, as we had booked a connecting flight to Christchurch that same day. But we quickly found out that our flight had been canceled because of the earthquake that had just happened in Christchurch. This time it was a big one, killing 185 people and injuring several thousand. We got a hotel for the night, and I was glued to the TV taking in the scenes as the news of the devastation unfolded.

The next day we were able to get on the first flight to Christchurch. Of all the flights I have been on over the years, there was something different about this one. It was quiet. Awkwardly quiet. But as the plane landed, I could hear several people sobbing. Some of them had been away, only to come back to rubble and uncertainty.

Earthquakes shake not only the earth but also our lives. This was the case for Taka and Rona, a young couple living in Christchurch. After the quake they were looking for answers. Where is God in all of this? What is the purpose of life? What does the future hold? They heard about the public Bible seminar we were having in the city, and started to attend. Not long afterward they both expressed their desire to get baptized, entering a new life with Jesus.

Today this couple help lead a vibrant church in the city, reaching more people who are also looking for answers in life.

Their journey started with an earthquake that shook their world, but it ended with a newfound stability and foundation. When everything shakes around us, we can plant our feet on the unmovable rock, Jesus Christ.

## TWO FOUNDATIONS

Jesus told the story of a wise man who built his house on a rock, while a foolish man built his house on sand. When the storm hit both homes, the one on the rock stood firm while the house on the sand collapsed.

*"'Therefore whoever hears these sayings of Mine, and does them, I will liken him to a wise man who built his house on the rock: and the*

rain descended, the floods came, and the winds blew and beat on that house; and it did not fall, for it was founded on the rock.

"'But everyone who hears these sayings of Mine, and does not do them, will be like a foolish man who built his house on the sand: and the rain descended, the floods came, and the winds blew and beat on that house; and it fell. And great was its fall.

"And so it was, when Jesus had ended these sayings, that the people were astonished at His teaching, for He taught them as one having authority, and not as the scribes" (Matthew 7:24-29).

In our final parable we will take a closer look at what it means to build on rock or on sand. Jesus is revealing that things we perhaps thought were solid and predictable in life are not providing the foundation we need when challenges come our way. Earthly security can give the illusion of a firm foundation, but we need something more lasting. We are all builders of our lives, and the question is what we have chosen as our foundation.

The parable of the wise and foolish builders appears at the end of the famous Sermon on the Mount and begins with the words *"Therefore whoever hears these sayings of Mine,"* which is an obvious reference back to the teachings contained in the sermon of Jesus. The wise person heeds the words of Jesus and lives by them.

There is also an immediate context with the teaching contained in the verses directly before this parable. Here Jesus is picturing those who profess to follow Him, but don't actually have a personal connection with Him.

Jesus says:

*"Not everyone who says to Me, 'Lord, Lord,' shall enter the kingdom of heaven, but he who does the will of My Father in heaven. Many will say to Me in that day, 'Lord, Lord, have we not prophesied in Your name, cast out demons in Your name, and done many wonders in Your name?' And then I will declare to them, 'I never knew you; depart from Me, you who practice lawlessness!' "* (verses 21-23).

Jesus describes those who boast knowing Him but are not

interested in practicing and following His law of life. Remember how the foolish builder in the parable hears the words of Jesus but does not do them.

However, from all outward appearances this group of people seems to be doing fine. They even claim having mighty experiences with God. It appears that Jesus is speaking to professed religious people here. The man who built his house on the sand heard the words of Jesus. The problem is not what he did not hear, but with what he did not do. Jesus is telling us that there is a stable and unstable foundation on which to construct our lives. It all comes down to whether we will be doers of His words.

Regardless of our intentions, it is possible to base our confidence and trust on what is insecure, like the shifting sand. The house the foolish man built represents a life seen in beliefs, convictions, aspirations, and choices. This can appear solid at first. The house can even consist of things that in themselves are not wrong, such as a job, marriage, health, and finances. We trust these things, and they give us stability in life. But take notice that all these things can change. We can lose our job and finances. A marriage can break, and our health can fail. Storms of life suddenly reveal that the stability we thought we had was an illusion if our lives are not built on something unchangeable.

## DIGGING DEEP

The rock represents Christ and the principles of His kingdom (1 Corinthians 10:4). He does not change, and when the storms of life hit us, His words, promises, mercy, forgiveness, and power remain.

In Matthew's account we are told that the man who builds his house on the rock is the man who heard the teachings of Jesus and lived according to them. He practiced what he heard.

Notice a detail Luke adds when he records the parable:

*"Whoever comes to Me, and hears My sayings and does them, I will show you whom he is like: He is like a man building a house, who dug*

*deep and laid the foundation on the rock. And when the flood arose, the stream beat vehemently against that house, and could not shake it, for it was founded on the rock"* (Luke 6:47, 48).

Luke mentions that the man dug deep to lay the foundation. Digging deep is the key here. We are invited, not just to hear the words of Jesus, but to dig into His teachings, seeking to make them the very stability and structure of our existence.

The wise builder is the one who comes to Jesus, listens to His words, explores His teachings, and then puts them into practice. This approach expresses great faith in the words of Jesus, as we acknowledge they are the very foundation of our lives. Building on the rock isn't a picture of being nominally religious or knowing Jesus from a distance. Being a true Christian means being a person who labors to establish his beliefs, choices, and view of the world on the truth of who Jesus is and what He has accomplished. This is someone who deeply cares about truth and sound doctrine. Someone who is not content with status quo, but longs for a deeper experience.

Another interesting observation in the parable is that the difference between the houses is only seen once the storm hits both houses. The foundation of the house on the rock was not visible. However, the outcome of the decision to dig deep was seen and noticed by all once the storm swept in. Challenges, calamities, trials, and difficulties sweep away the superficial and reveal what is lasting. The testimony of the Christian is not that he or she does not experience tough times. Our testimony lies in the strength of our foundation in the person Jesus. We know where to go to find peace amid a storm. Jesus brings out in the parable that it is in our best interest to build on the rock. This is because He knows that He has what it takes to endure the storms that will inevitably hit all of us in this fallen world.

Digging deep is a work that takes place on the inside of us. Jesus fills us with His precious promises. We believe that what He has said He is also able to accomplish.

## TRUSTING GOD'S PROMISES

One of the most beautiful definitions of faith is found in Romans. It is said of Abraham:

*"He did not waver at the promise of God through unbelief, but was strengthened in faith, giving glory to God, and being fully convinced that what He had promised He was also able to* perform. *And therefore 'it was accounted to him for righteousness' "* (Romans 4:20-22).

Are you fully convinced that what God can do what He said He can do? And to make it more personal: are you fully convinced that He can fulfill His promises in your life?

This is where the rubber meets the road. It's when concepts become real. When theory becomes practical, and God's promises suddenly take on a life of their own. They are seen in the experience of people who walk by faith.

Abraham's faith was not just a philosophy. When God asked him to pack up and go to a land He would show him, he actually moved, while not even knowing how it would all end. Sometimes we don't always fully understand everything until we have taken a step in faith. This is where trust plays such an important role in the Christian life. God asks us to trust His Word and make it the guide of our lives.

## A JOURNEY OF FAITH

One of my favorite chapters in Scripture is Hebrews 11. It is known as the faith chapter. Starting at the dawn of time, it traces individuals throughout the scriptural narrative who trusted God and acted on their convictions.

The interesting thing about all these personalities is that although they have their faith in God in common, their lives are all unique. Faith plays itself out in our lives in different ways.

The first person mentioned in Hebrews 11 is Abel:

*"By faith Abel offered to God a more excellent sacrifice than Cain, through which he obtained witness that he was righteous, God testifying of his gifts; and through it he being dead still speaks"* (verse 4).

Abel was persecuted and killed by his brother Cain. He died

for his faith.

The second person we are introduced to in Hebrews 11 is Enoch:

*"By faith Enoch was taken away so that he did not see death, 'and was not found, because God had taken him'; for before he was taken he had this testimony, that he pleased God"* (verse 5).

Enoch never tasted death. Because of his faith, he was rewarded with life. Eternal life!

So does living by faith lead to death or life? Obviously, both are possible. Faith unfolds itself in different ways in different people. But both the lives of Abel and Enoch are marked by faithfulness.

This seems to be an ongoing theme in Hebrews 11.

Next in line is Noah:

*"By faith Noah, being divinely warned of things not yet seen, moved with godly fear, prepared an ark for the saving of his household, by which he condemned the world and became heir of the righteousness which is according to faith"* (verse 7).

When you are going to build a boat, you need to stick around in one place for a while. Noah built and preached for many years, warning the world of a coming flood.

But then the very next verse in Hebrews 11 introduces us to Abraham:

*"By faith Abraham obeyed when he was called to go out to the place which he would receive as an inheritance. And he went out, not knowing where he was going"* (verse 8).

Abraham is asked to pack up and move.

So is faith staying or moving? Again, we must answer: both!

I don't know exactly what God is asking you to do. All I know is that you will need faith to do it. Our lives are all unique, with their own challenges and blessings woven into the great tapestry of God's story. Our individual story is to become a part of His greater narrative.

In a sense we can say that Hebrews 11 is an unfinished chapter. I know it has 40 verses in our Bibles, but in reality there are far more verses. God knows the whole story because He is the one writing it, and He wants you and me to be part of this incredible narrative of faith.

## DEFEAT AND VICTORY

Perhaps you are thinking that you are not good enough to join this story. But the fascinating thing about Hebrews 11 is that it doesn't list infallible heroes, but rather faulty people who, understanding their weaknesses, put their trust in God. They were not strong in themselves, but received strength from above.

Samson, David, and Rahab are among those who are listed in Hebrews 11. If you know anything about these individuals, you're aware that they had their weak moments. At times they built on sand. And when the storms of life hit, they were almost swept away. But thank God for the "almost" part. Because the God of the Scriptures is a God of new opportunities.

Sometimes we need to hit rock bottom to discover the Rock!

Charles Spurgeon, A famous preacher from the nineteenth century, once said: *"I have learned to kiss the waves that throw me up against the Rock of Ages."* Trials can even be blessings in disguise, that make us cling more to Jesus.

I like to think of Hebrews 11 as the active memory of God. I am not implying that God forgets anything, but there are things He chooses to remember and focus on. Our lives consist of ups and downs, victories and defeats, joys and sorrows. Through it all God is with us—encouraging us and pointing us to the source of our strength, His Word. He cherishes the moments we cling to Him and put our faith and trust in His promises.

Hebrews 11 is like God's family photo album, full of pictures of what faith looks like. Each life is a portrait of grace, a depiction of God's strength being made perfect in our weakness (2 Corinthians 12:9).

Paul once referred to the apostles as *"a spectacle to the world, both to angels and to men"* (1 Corinthians 4:9).

What a thought! All the universe, full of heavenly beings, is watching this world like a theater. Our lives are being closely followed by unfallen angels.

Luke asks the question:

*"When the Son of Man comes, will He really find faith on the earth?"* (Luke 18:8).

I think He will. I know He will.

Because there are individuals like you who hear the teachings of Jesus and want to build your life on His words.

## WHAT MATTERS MOST

In the Gospel of John we read about how Jesus miraculously fed more than 5,000 people with five barley loaves and two small fish. The crowds are excited and wonder if perhaps the promised Messiah has shown up at last. They flock to hear Jesus the next day and require another miracle. However, Jesus knew their hearts and that unfortunately many had come only for temporal food. They had not yet tasted the bread that had come from heaven.

Jesus points to what matters most:

*"For the bread of God is He who comes down from heaven and gives life to the world"* (John 6:33).

*"I am the bread of life. He who comes to Me shall never hunger, and he who believes in Me shall never thirst. But I said to you that you have seen Me and yet do not believe"* (verses 35, 36).

Many were offended at His words. They were looking for a different kind of Messiah. The kingdom that Jesus proclaimed was simply not attractive to them. Many left that day.

We encounter one of the saddest verses in Scripture:

*"From that time many of His disciples went back and walked with Him no more"* (verse 66).

Can you picture the scene in your mind? Multitudes are walking away from the very One who has the words of life. They choose to build on the sand of earthly security instead of the rock of eternal safety. It just seemed the easier thing to do right there, after Jesus came with some challenging and hard sayings. Building on sand is definitely easier and quicker than building on rock. And when we add a little peer pressure into the mix, the "sand builders" win the majority.

But there will be those who are willing to swim against the stream of popular opinion. Among the crowds there will be individuals who grasp the kingdom of God and pursue it with all their strength.

## TO WHOM SHALL WE GO?

As the multitudes walk away, Jesus addresses His closest disciples.

*"Then Jesus said to the twelve, "Do you also want to go away?"* (verse 67).

Impulsive Peter is the first to answer. He is the kind of person who often either says things that are totally off or absolutely nails it.

On one occasion he is with Jesus on a mountain, and a great light surrounds Jesus, as He converses with Elijah and Moses. Peter comes up with an idea: *"Master, it is good for us to be here; and let us make three tabernacles: one for You, one for Moses, and one for Elijah."* Luke adds, insightfully, *"not knowing what he said"* (Luke 9:33).

But after Jesus asks: *"Do you also want to go away,"* Peter hits an absolute home run with his answer.

*"But Simon Peter answered Him, 'Lord, to whom shall we go? You have the words of eternal life. Also, we have come to believe and know that You are the Christ, the Son of the living God' "* (John 6:68, 69).

Wow! Amazing! Thanks, Peter!

He was so right. Jesus has the words of eternal life! He is our Rock.

To whom else shall we go?

Life's storms will at times confront us with fear, uncertainty, and doubt. There will be valleys in our Christian experience that will be challenging to pass through. We might even be tempted to give up.

But an honest survey of the options that seek to provide answers to the deepest human questions will result in the cry of Peter: *"To whom shall we go?"*

There is no worldview, ideology, or other religion that even comes close to offering what Jesus provides.

Only in Him we find our true value and purpose!

And so our journey together ends. It's my prayer that the parables that we looked at may be like pillars in your life. Monuments of God's goodness, grace, and truth.

Parables have a way of ingraining themselves in our minds. These stories of transformation contain mental images that stick. They are etched into our consciousness, ready to be recalled when needed.

So whenever you see a seed, may you be reminded of the power of God's Word. When you think of a treasure, may you think of Jesus. Every time you stand on a rock, may you be reminded to stand on God's promises. When you pass a vineyard, may you remember that God has a place for you in His gospel work. And the next time you see a bridal couple, uniting their lives on their wedding day, may you know that Jesus is your bridegroom who is soon coming to take you home.

There will come a day when you will be embraced by the arms who were stretched on Calvary to save you.

We will see Him face-to-face!

It will not be a dream or a vision. It will not be a metaphor or a concept. It will not be a type or a shadow.

And it will not be a parable.

It will be Him. Jesus.